GW00697116

PSA Services

National Schedule of Rates

National Schedule of Rates Landscape Management

London: HMSO

First published 1991

ISBN 0 11 671549 9

USER NOTES:

....
....
....
....
....
....
....
....
....
....
....
....
....
....
....
....
....
....
....
....
....
....
....
....
....
....

Foreword

This Schedule of Rates has been jointly sponsored by PSA Services and the National Schedule of Rates for use in both the public and private sectors.

This is the first Schedule of Rates to be jointly published by the PSA and the NSR and it is hoped that it will produce benefits for both clients and contractors concerned with landscape management. The views of users would be welcome.

A full back-up service is provided to give advice and assistance together with the opportunity to obtain further specialist services for all aspects of landscape management.

Feedback from users is encouraged and will be evaluated for possible inclusion in future editions.

Contents

A: General Directions

GENERALLY

Preambles

Preambles which apply to all Sections are contained in this General Directions Section.

Preambles which only apply to specific Sections and Sub-sections are contained within the particular Section.

Tender documents

The Conditions of Contract and all other tender documents are to be read in conjunction with this Schedule.

Legislation

Comply with all relevant legislation current at the time of execution of the work.

PRELIMINARIES

All Inclusive Rates

The Rates in this Schedule are all inclusive and, as such, include for Preliminaries.

Significant preliminary items

When assessing any adjustment to be tendered to the level of the Rates, consideration must be given to any unique preliminary items which could be encountered. The following list gives examples only and does not limit the actual requirements encountered:

Establishment charges, overheads and profit.
Nature and location of the Works.
Liabilities and insurances.
Access to the Works.
Existing services.
Plant, tools, vehicles and transport.
Site organisation, security, health and safety.
Water, lighting and power.
Temporary works: eg hardstandings, accommodation, storage, telephones, fencing, footways and gantries.
Statutory obligations.

Value of old items

Unless specifically agreed otherwise, all old items for disposal will become the sole property of the Contractor.

Removing and depositing arisings

Unless specifically agreed otherwise, all arisings for removing and depositing will become the sole property of the Employer.

Materials and workmanship

Where not particularly specified, materials and methods of working are at the Contractor's discretion and must be entirely suitable and of good practice for the work in hand.

Materials paid for separately

Reimbursement of the cost of materials, unless the Conditions of Contract state otherwise, will be made on the basis of agreed current market or invoice rates delivered to site or store (after the deduction of all discounts obtainable for cash, insofar as they exceed $2^1/_2$ per cent, and of all trade discounts, rebates and allowances) with the addition of 5 per cent to cover profit and all other liabilities. Such reimbursement shall not be subject to further adjustment.

Sub-contractors and Suppliers

In the case of work ordered to be placed with a Sub-Contractor or Supplier, the Contractor, unless the Conditions of Contract state otherwise, will be reimbursed the net agreed amount of their account (after the deduction of all discounts obtainable for cash, insofar as they exceed $2^1/_2$ per cent, and of all trade discounts, rebates and allowances) with the addition of 5 per cent to cover profit and all other liabilities. Such reimbursement shall not be subject to further adjustment.

ENVIRONMENTAL PROTECTION

Generally

All operations are to be strictly controlled to avoid contamination of soil, ground water, waterways, wildlife habitats, etc. Comply with all legislative controls and regulations to this end.

Fire risk

During periods of high fire risk, ensure that any activity carried out does not increase that risk.

PLANT, EQUIPMENT AND TOOLS

Generally

To be of approved type, appropriate to the work ordered and maintained and operated in accordance with the manufacturer's instructions and relevant Codes of Practice.

Maintenance

Carry out refuelling and servicing of machines on paved, not grassed, bitumen or tarmac areas.

Clean up spilled fuel, oil, etc immediately with suitable solvents.

Immobilise or remove from site all machines at the end of each working day.

Tractors

When used for grass cutting, maintenance work or where otherwise specified, tractors are to be fitted with grassland tyres. Do not operate on sloping ground with a gradient exceeding that recommended by the vehicle manufacturer.

'Ride-on' self-powered equipment

Do not operate on sloping ground with a gradient exceeding that recommended by the manufacturer.

DEFINITIONS

Superintending Officer (SO)

The person appointed by the Employer as his representative.

Approved, directed or ordered

Approved, directed or ordered by the SO.

Or equivalent

Alternative articles and materials to those described and approved by the SO in writing.

BS

The latest British Standard (published by the British Standards Institution) referred to by its serial number, including any amendments, revisions or replacements or the equivalent national standard of any Member State of the European Community, or any equivalent international standard recognised in such a Member State.

Site

The land or place where work is to be executed and any adjacent land or place which may be used to carry out work.

Store

A permanent or temporary structure providing security and weather protection for storage purposes within or in close proximity to the site.

Masonry (as a background for fixing)

Includes concrete, brick, block or stone.

Timber (as a background for fixing)

Includes all forms of timber and manufactured building board, etc.

Large stones

Stones exceeding 50 mm in any dimension.

Obstructions

Airfield lights, manhole covers, trees or the like.

Small area

Area not exceeding 2500 square metres.

Large area

Area exceeding 2500 square metres.

Confined area

Area of work not exceeding 2500 square metres bounded on three or more sides by obstructions which will not permit the machines and equipment to manoeuvre freely.

Isolated area

Area of work not exceeding 2500 square metres which requires the separate transportation of equipment.

METHOD OF MEASUREMENT

Measurement rules

This Schedule stands alone. Where not self-evident from the Item descriptions, the rules of measurement are stated.

Measurement

Generally:
Measure work net as executed unless otherwise stated.

Where Rates are quoted per 100 m, per 100 m^2 or per hectare: take dimensions used in calculating quantities to the nearest 500 mm.

All other Rates: take dimensions used in calculating quantities to the nearest 10 mm.

Voids:
Unless otherwise stated, minimum deductions for voids refer only to openings or wants within the boundaries of the measured work.

Always deduct openings or wants at the boundaries of measured work, irrespective of size.

Do not measure Items for widths not exceeding a stated limit where these widths are caused by voids.

Lineal or superficial work on sloping or undulating sites:
Measure on the surface of the ground.

Excavating and subsequent disposal:
Measure the bulk before excavating and make no allowance for any subsequent variations in bulk.

Filling:
Measure as equal to the void filled.

Measure thickness after compaction.

Nominal sizes

All sizes are nominal unless otherwise stated.

Size ranges

Sizes expressed as ".... to ....", are to be read as "exceeding .... but not exceeding ....".

Billing

Bill all quantities to the nearest two decimal places of the billing unit for each particular Item.

RATES

Base date

The Rates in this Schedule reflect the costs of resources as at the first quarter 1991.

Multiplying factors

Where two or more multiplying factors are to be applied to a Rate, the factors are first to be multiplied together and not added.

Rates expressed per unit of thickness, weight, volume etc

Rates per unit of thickness, width, girth, or the like:
Pay for part of a unit as a whole unit.

Rates expressed per unit of weight or of volume per unit of area:
(eg per tonne per hectare, per m^3 per hectare) Calculate the Rate proportionally for the actual weight or volume.

Work in confined areas or isolated areas:

Where the unit of measurement is the Hectare (except for Stone Picking (Items C23 and C24) and Litter Clearance (Item F93)), *multiply the appropriate Rates by 1.50.*

Rates throughout exclude (except where otherwise stated)

Drawings:
Preparing drawings.

Rates throughout include (except where otherwise stated)

All Rates:
For preliminaries, labour, waste and lost time.

For supplying and delivering materials unless described as paid for separately.

For taking delivery, unloading materials and getting into store or other approved position.

For storage of materials.

For transporting to the site, assembling, fitting and fixing materials in position.

For carrying out work in any circumstances, unless otherwise stated. It is assumed that work carried out in disadvantageous circumstances will be offset by work carried out in advantageous circumstances.

For carrying out the work in accordance with the requirements of the Specification clauses whether or not these requirements are repeated elsewhere.

For executing in sections as necessitated by the nature of the work or to suit the chosen method of working.

For any break in working after the continuity of the work has been interrupted by any temporary obstruction not specifically stated in this Schedule.

For providing all equipment, implements and tools.

For multiple handling materials and items.

For providing samples and tests.

For protecting old and new works from damage.

For square cutting.

For fixing to new or old backgrounds.

For providing all necessary dust sheets and tarpaulin coverings to protect adjacent work.

For laying dust by sprinkling with water.

For keeping the site free from all surplus materials, rubbish and debris arising from the execution of the Works.

Generally:
For watching and lighting and for providing barriers, notices, signals, flagmen etc to regulate traffic flow as necessary.

Sowing grass seed:
For sowing at a minimum coverage rate of 35 g/m^2.

Taking out, taking up or the like:
For breaking up, cutting away, stripping or the like.

For removing off the site to a shoot or other place of disposal including payment of any charges in connection therewith.

For removing to stack or other place of storage on the site as ordered.

For carefully taking out all materials ordered to be stacked or removed to store for re-use.

For carefully taking out all fixings both from the background and from the item removed.

For all necessary cleaning of materials removed to store in preparation for re-use.

For all necessary dismantling of bulky fittings or the like preparatory to removing to stack or store.

Fixing only or laying only:
For fixing only or laying only new items or items previously set aside for re-use.

For taking delivery, storing and sending back returnable packings.

For obtaining from stack or other place of storage on site.

For handling, loading, unloading, protecting, transporting to the site, hoisting, lowering, assembling and fixing complete.

For all fixing or jointing materials required.

Work in repairs:
For removing any existing work.

For new work to match existing.

For all preparatory work and making good.

For jointing new to existing work.

For work of any width.

Composite items:
For assembling, breaking down into suitable sections for transport and installation and subsequent reassembly and any adjustment necessary for fixing.

Plugging:
For providing and fixing approved proprietary plugs or, at the Contractor's discretion, for fixing by approved mechanical means.

Work to crossfalls:
For intersections.

Removing and depositing:
For collecting, loading, transporting within the boundary of the site and depositing.

Burning:
For burning on site where directed and providing all supervision.

Disposing:
For collecting, loading and transporting to a place of disposal outside the boundary of the site including payment of any charges in connection therewith.

Work involving the use of wheeled equipment:
For manoeuvering to clear obstructions.

Work executed by means other than tractors:
For work to sloping ground, banks and traverses except where specifically indicated in this Schedule of Rates.

Work executed with tractors:
For work to sloping ground having a gradient not exceeding 18° from the horizontal.

B: Clearance

GENERALLY

Specification

Before commencing work, verify with the SO which shrubs, hedges and trees are to be retained.

Tools: keep sharp and properly set.

Method of measurement

Girths of trees and saplings:
Measure at a height of 1.00 m above ground level.

Notes

Supplying imported filling material:
Pay for separately.

Rates for the following include

Filling voids:
For using selected material obtained from elsewhere on the site, or approved imported material as ordered.

VEGETATION

Method of Measurement

Clearing grass, etc on or against fencing:
Measure the length of the fence.

Rates for the following include

Clearing site:
For removing hedges, trees and saplings not exceeding 150 mm girth where in massed growth or within an area of bushes, scrub or undergrowth.

Item		1	2 ADD for burning arisings	3 ADD for disposing arisings
	100 Square Metres	£	£	£
	Clearing site: removing and depositing arisings: cultivating surface to even gradient and medium tilth			
B1	bracken, light undergrowth or the like	28.94	3.13	9.43
B2	bushes, scrub and undergrowth	149.10	9.40	37.72
B3	ADD for grubbing up roots: filling voids left by removal of roots	118.43	2.09	6.29
B4	Cutting down brambles: pulling or grubbing up roots: removing and depositing arisings	22.67	2.61	7.88
	Metre			
	Clearing grass and other vegetation growing on or against fencing: pulling or grubbing up roots: removing and depositing arisings			
B5	one side of fence	0.63	0.05	0.15
B6	both sides of fence	1.04	0.08	0.25

HEDGES, TREES AND SHRUBS

Specification

Tree felling:

a. Carry out in accordance with BS 3998 and current Forestry Safety Council guides, using only skilled labour.
b. Trees not exceeding 250 mm girth: remove complete with roots.
c. Trees exceeding 250 mm girth: cut down to ground level. Trees felled in confined spaces are to be taken down in sections using ropes to lower timber.

Stack cordwood and felled timber (where to be retained) in neat piles where directed.

Stump grinding: to 150 mm below ground level or as directed.

Kill stumps with chemicals applied in accordance with the manufacturer's recommendations.

Fill voids left by removal of trees or stump grinding. Consolidate to level of adjacent ground. Where ordered cultivate surface to a fine tilth to form seed bed and sow grass seeds at the coverage rate directed.

Notes

Supplying grass seed:
Pay for separately.

Rates for the following include

Cutting down hedges:
For trees and saplings not exceeding 150 mm girth in the run of the hedge.

Item	*Metre*	1	2	3
		Height of hedge		
		not exceeding 1.50 m	1.50 to 2.00 m	2.00 to 3.00 m
		£	£	£
	Cutting down: grubbing up roots: filling voids left by removal of roots: removing and depositing arisings			
B7	hedge	5.29	6.85	9.98
	ADD for			
B8	burning arisings	0.45	0.55	0.75
B9	disposing arisings	1.05	1.55	2.65

Item	*Each*	1	2	3
			ADD for burning arisings	ADD for disposing arisings
		£	£	£
	tree or shrub: not exceeding 250 mm girth			
B10	500 to 1000 mm high: 2000 mm spread	1.30	0.20	0.60
B11	1000 to 1500 mm high: 3000 mm spread	2.73	0.25	0.95
B12	1500 to 2000 mm high: 4000 mm spread	8.19	0.40	1.30
B13	2000 to 3000 mm high: 5000 mm spread	9.56	0.55	1.65
B14	exceeding 3000 mm high: exceeding 5000 mm spread	10.92	0.70	2.10

Item	Each	1	2	3	4
		Girth			
		250 to 600 mm	600 to 900 mm	900 to 1200 mm	1200 to 1500 mm
		£	£	£	£
B15	Cutting down mature tree: removing and depositing arisings	49.10	62.55	89.40	139.90
	ADD for				
B16	burning arisings	0.91	3.90	6.50	13.00
B17	disposing arisings	2.65	6.50	19.50	32.50
B18	Chemically killing tree stump	2.60	3.90	5.20	6.50
B19	Grinding tree stump to 150 mm below ground level: filling void: removing and depositing arisings	5.60	7.46	9.42	11.39
	ADD for				
B20	burning arisings	0.52	0.78	1.04	1.30
B21	disposing arisings	1.04	1.43	1.69	2.08
B22	Grubbing up stump and roots of tree: filling void: depositing arisings	7.60	10.62	16.50	20.95
	ADD for				
B23	burning arisings	0.65	0.91	1.17	1.56
B24	disposing arisings	1.17	1.56	1.95	2.47

Item	*Square Metre*	£
B25	Cultivating and sowing grass seed where roots of hedge, tree or shrub removed	0.10

C: Preparation of Land

GENERALLY

Specification

Standards: carry out the work to approved agricultural and horticultural standards.

Timing: time all stages of work to obtain optimum effect, giving full regard to the season, weather and soil condition.

Cultivate soil to depths stated or as otherwise ordered. Carry out the work using ploughs, disc harrows, rotary cultivators, rigid or spring tined harrows or other equipment as ordered. Produce a coarse friable soil condition to the full working depth suitable for blade grading.

Subsoiling to break up deep panning may be carried out as part of the soil cultivation if ordered.

Blade grading will normally follow cultivation. Obtain approval to the work before proceeding with the final stage of preparation.

Final preparation of the land: carry out with cultivators, harrows and rollers to an approved firmness and grade of tilth. When ordered, the final preparation and sowing of grass seed is to be carried out using a combined harrow, tilther and seeder.

Finish of beds for seeding is to:

a. Conform to the levels ordered with the surface free from large stones or the like.

b. Consist of the correct crumb structure to the full working depth with a fine tilth to a depth of 25 mm to approval.

Finish of beds for turf: same as that for seeding *except* that the surface is to be consolidated and finished to a tilth approximately 12 mm deep to approval.

Note

Clearing vegetation:
Pay for separately.

Rates for the following include

Generally:
For work executed using equipment mounted on or towed by tractor, unless otherwise stated.

For clearing obstructions to the use of equipment before commencing the work.

For disposing roots and all weeds.

For stone picking *except* where work is paid for at Rates per Hectare when Items C23 to C25 shall be paid in addition.

For work on any type of soil.

Ploughing, cultivating, harrowing and rolling:
For once over the area ordered.

PLOUGHING

Specification

Ploughs: suitable for the depth of cultivation ordered.

Furrows: of even depth and uniform finish with vegetation turned in and buried.

Depth and type of ploughing: as ordered.

Rates for the following include

Ploughing:
For ploughing arable, stubble or grassland.

Item	*Hectare*	£
	Ploughing	
C1	not exceeding 150 mm deep	65.00
C2	150 to 250 mm deep	76.70

SUBSOILING

Specification

Break up compacted subsoil or plough pan on arable or grassland by subsoiling not exceeding 750 mm deep as directed.

Roll the surface of grassed areas with a smooth roller after subsoiling.

Item		£
	100 Metres	
C3	Breaking up subsoil	1.43

HARROWING

Specification

Harrow with the equipment ordered to produce a coarse crumb structure to the depth required or to produce a fine crumb tilth as directed.

Item		£
	Hectare	
	Harrowing: using	
C4	chain or light flexible spiked harrow	9.10
C5	drag harrow	18.20
C6	standard disc harrow	27.30
C7	heavy disc harrow	35.10
C8	spring tined harrow	29.90
C9	heavy rigid tined ripper harrow	41.60
C10	tractor-mounted heavy rotary cultivator	33.80
	100 Square Metres	
C11	Cultivating: with pedestrian operated self-powered rotary cultivator on small area	9.10

ROLLING CULTIVATED LAND

Specification

Rollers: tractor-drawn general-purpose smooth or Cambridge ring type as ordered.

Speed: operate at a speed that will produce the optimum crushing of clods and degree of consolidation ordered but not to exceed 10 km/h.

Small cultivated areas: rolling speed is not to exceed 3 km/h.

Item	*Hectare*	£
	Rolling: using	
C12	three-gang roller	9.75
C13	single-section roller	16.90
	100 Square Metres	
	Rolling small cultivated area: using	
C14	hand roller	2.08
C15	pedestrian operated self-powered roller	0.98

CULTIVATING AND GRASS SEEDING

Note

Supplying grass seed:
Pay for separately.

	Hectare	£
C16	Cultivating and sowing approved grass seed at rate directed: using tractor-mounted combined harrow, tilther and seeder	29.25

MINOR GRADING

Specification

Timing: carry out work only when soil is dry enough to maintain crumb structure to the full working depth.

Machine grading:
Finish the work so that:

a. Final levels are to the standard of accuracy ordered.
b. Work marries in to adjoining arable or grass land after settlement.
c. Work adjoining runways, roads and kerbs or the like coincides with the gradients of their surfaces. Allow for settlement so that the final levels are 35 mm above the adjoining hard surfaces.
d. The finished surface is uniformly smooth and free of sudden changes in levels, within tolerances ordered and sufficiently even to allow the range of equipment used in its maintenance to work easily at normal operating speeds without damage to the equipment or the turf.

Hand grading:
Finish the work so that:

a. Work marries in to adjoining grass surfaces after settlement.
b. Work adjoining hard surfaces is not less than 25 mm proud of such surfaces after settlement.
c. The finished surface consists of a uniformly fine tilth, consolidated by heeling to an even degree as ordered.

Equipment:
For large areas use tractor-drawn wheeled blade graders.

For small areas use tractor-mounted blades not exceeding 1.5 m wide or other approved equipment as appropriate.

Note

The Items in this Sub-section apply only where the adjustment of existing levels does not involve any increase or decrease exceeding 150 mm.

MINOR GRADING

Item	*Hectare*	£
C17	Machine grading large area	35.10
	100 Square Metres	
C18	Machine grading small area	0.39
C19	Hand grading small area	16.25

HAND DIGGING AND RAKING

Rates for the following include

Digging and raking:
For collecting weeds (together with roots) and large stones or the like: disposing and leaving area tidy.

Item	*100 Square Metres*	£
C20	Digging with spade to an average depth of 230 mm: leaving rough	31.35
C21	Digging with fork or spade to an average depth of 230 mm: breaking down lumps: leaving surface with a medium tilth	34.50
C22	Hand raking dug or graded soil: breaking down lumps to a fine tilth: leaving surface smooth and even	6.27

STONE PICKING

Definition

Other extraneous debris:
Anything lying on the surface which might damage grass cutting equipment or vehicle tyres, or which might be a hazard to aircraft.

Item	*Hectare*	£
	Picking up by hand exposed large stones and other extraneous debris on cultivated area: gathering into piles: removing and depositing	
C23	not exceeding 0.5 m^3 per hectare	24.70
C24	0.5 to 1 m^3 per hectare	29.90
C25	ADD for disposing—*per m^3 per hectare*	11.38

D: Soft Landscaping

EXCAVATING AND SPREADING SOIL

Specification

Imported soil (where ordered):
Quantity and quality as ordered.

Obtain from an approved supplier.

Spilt soil: take care that soil is not spilt on to roadways or the like. Clean up as necessary.

Definition

Recently deposited soil:
Soil deposited in temporary soil heaps not exceeding six months prior to the execution of the order, and includes:

a. Material from a source other than the excavations.
b. Material deposited under a separate order or contract.
c. Material from the excavations which, in the opinion of the SO, is impossible to deposit in readiness for spreading and levelling.

Note

Imported soil (where ordered):
Pay for separately.

Rates for the following include

Generally:
For hand or machine work *except* where otherwise stated.

Item	*Cubic Metre*	£
	Excavating	
	recently deposited soil: loading: transporting a distance not exceeding 1 km: depositing ready for spreading	
D1	excavating by machine ...	3.25
D2	excavating by hand ...	7.15
	other than recently deposited soil from bank, soil heap or consolidated ground: loading: transporting a distance not exceeding 1 km: depositing ready for spreading	
D3	excavating by machine ...	3.90
D4	excavating by hand ...	8.19
	screened soil: loading: transporting a distance not exceeding 1 km: depositing, spreading and grading not exceeding 25 mm thick: working into surface of ground	
D5	by machine ...	9.62
D6	by hand: using 'Trulute' or other approved implement ...	14.43
D7	ADD to Items D1 to D6 *for each additional 0.5 km of transporting distance* ...	0.65
D8	recently deposited soil: filling into wheelbarrows: wheeling a distance not exceeding 50 m: depositing ready for spreading ...	9.62
D9	selected top soil from spoil heap: passing through mechanical screen of approved gauge: removing and depositing screenings ...	11.57
D10	ADD for disposing screenings ...	0.65
	Spreading and grading deposited soil in layers	
D11	not exceeding 100 mm thick ...	1.43
D12	100 to 200 mm thick ...	1.37

BANK STABILISATION AND PEST CONTROL

Specification

Mesh and fixing pins or pegs: obtain from an approved manufacturer.

a. Polypropylene/wire mesh:
   1. mesh size: 8 No 8 mm threads per 100 mm.
   2. weight: 0.20 kg/m^2.
   3. fixing pins: 203 mm long.

b. Polyethylene composite mesh in four layers:
   1. weight: 0.45 kg/m^2.
   2. fixing pegs: 280 mm long.

Lay:

a. Polypropylene/wire mesh:
   1. side and end laps: 80 mm.
   2. fixing pins: at 500 mm centres along all edges.

b. Polyethylene composite mesh:
   1. side and end laps: 100 mm.
   2. fixing pegs at 1000 mm centres along all edges.

Drive pegs well into ground so that no projections will interfere with mowing.

Bury edge of mesh:

a. where abutting retaining walls or the like: turn down edge and bury 150 mm deep into ground; secure with fixing pins or pegs.

b. at perimeter: turn down edge and bury 250 to 300 mm deep into ground; secure with fixing pins or pegs.

Notes

Covering mesh with top soil:
Where ordered, pay for at the appropriate Rates in the 'Excavating and Spreading Soil' Sub-Section.

Grass cutting prior to laying mesh:
Where ordered, pay for at the appropriate Rates in the 'Maintenance of Grassed Areas' Section.

Rates for the following include

Generally:
For work to banks, slopes, traverses, etc.

For laps.

For cutting to slope or profile.

For the use of ladders and planks on slopes exceeding 50° from horizontal.

Turning down and burying edge of mesh:
For all necessary excavation, temporary storage of spoil, backfilling, levelling and consolidation.

Item	*Square Metre*	1 Poly-propylene/ wire mesh £	2 Polyethylene composite mesh £
	Stabilising/pest control mesh: on grassed or soiled area:		
D13	on surfaces not exceeding 30° from horizontal	2.02	4.85
	on surfaces 30° to 50° from horizontal		
D14	not exceeding 2 m high	2.09	4.91
D15	2 to 5 m high	2.13	4.96
D16	5 to 10 m high	2.19	5.01
D17	exceeding 10 m high	2.23	5.06
	on surfaces exceeding 50° from horizontal		
D18	not exceeding 2 m high	2.33	5.16
D19	2 to 5 m high	2.44	5.26
D20	5 to 10 m high	2.55	5.36
D21	exceeding 10 m high	2.66	5.46
	Metre		
	Turning down and burying edge of mesh		
D22	at abutments to retaining walls or the like	0.85	0.95
D23	at perimeter	1.35	1.45

E: Turfing and Grass Seeding

STRIPPING AND LAYING TURF

Specification

Turves: comply with BS 3969.

Before turf stripping commences cut grass and roll as ordered.

Weather conditions: do not strip or lay turf when weather is exceptionally dry, when surfaces are waterlogged or during frost or snow.

Re-lay turf within 7 days of stripping. Ensure that the programme of stripping is co-ordinated with that of re-laying.

Stripping turf: cut and strip turf with turf float or mechanical stripper to a size of 900 × 300 × 30 mm thick. Roll up, remove and stack turf where directed not exceeding 1 m high. Box to an even thickness of 20 mm where ordered.

Turf bed: do not lay turf until bed has been brought to an approved degree of tilth and firmness. Dress with fertilizer as ordered.

Protection: do not drive vehicles or machines over prepared areas. Unload turf outside the area and provide access to the area being turfed by means of planked wheelbarrow runs.

Lay turf on prepared surface: bed level or not exceeding 30° from horizontal commencing on one side facing the unturfed area and working from the newly laid turf. Lay turves to stretcher bond with maximum stagger, closely butted and to correct falls.

Lay turf on prepared surface: 30° to 50° from horizontal using timber ladders and planks to ensure safe and efficient working. Lay turves diagonally or horizontally and secure with pointed wooden pegs 200 mm long or with 4 mm galvanised wire pins bent or hairpin pattern at least 200 mm long.

Turf beaters and rollers: do not use.

Adjust any deviation from specified levels by lifting turves, raking out or infilling with finely sifted soil and re-bed the turves.

Dress surface of the newly laid turf with dry finely sifted soil ensuring that after brushing in, all joints between turves are filled and leaving the surface with an approved level finish.

Water-in where so ordered, taking care that soil is not washed out of joints.

Notes

Fertilizing:
When ordered, pay for at the appropriate Rates in the 'Fertilizers, Pesticides and Top Dressing' Section.

Grass cutting:
When ordered, pay for at the appropriate Rates in the 'Maintenance of Grassed Areas' Section.

Supplying new turves:
Pay for separately.

STRIPPING AND LAYING TURF

Item	*Square Metre*	£
	Rolling, stripping, lifting and rolling up turf: transporting a distance not exceeding 1 km: stacking: stripping	
E1	by hand	0.52
E2	by mechanical turf-stripping equipment	0.33
E3	ADD *for each additional 1 km of transporting distance*	0.07
	Taking turf from stack: transporting a distance not exceeding 100 m: laying: dressing: on surface	
E4	level or not exceeding 30° from horizontal	0.52
	30° to 50° from horizontal	
E5	not exceeding 2 m high	0.52
E6	2 to 5 m high	0.72
E7	5 to 10 m high	1.56
E8	exceeding 10 m high	2.21
E9	Boxing and cutting turf to a uniform thickness of 20 mm: removing and depositing surplus material	0.33

GRASS SEEDING

GENERALLY

Specification

Seeds: named cultivars of certified EEC 'Blue Label' quality and within the supplier's time limit. Mixtures of seeds as ordered. Uncertified seeds will not be accepted.

Timing: sow seeds only when weather and soil conditions are approved.

Sowing: sow seeds either by hand or using mechanical seed sower in two passes, each at right angles to the other, or as otherwise directed. On large areas, harrow in seeds with light harrow and roll with smooth or ribbed roller. On small areas sow seeds evenly by hand, rake in and roll with light hand roller.

Notes

Harrowing and rolling:
Pay for at the appropriate Rates in the 'Preparation of Land' Section.

Supplying grass seeds:
Pay for separately.

Rates for the following include

Sowing:
For sowing at the coverage rates ordered.

SOWING GRASS SEED

Item	Description	£
	Hectare	
	Sowing grass seed	
E10	in two passes using mechanical seed sower	15.60
	100 Square Metres	
E11	by hand	3.13

REPAIRING DAMAGED GRASSED AREAS

Specification

Topsoil filling: fill with imported topsoil or topsoil from elsewhere on the site.

Notes

Topsoil filling: Pay for at the appropriate Rates in the 'Soft Landscaping' Section.

Item	*Square Metre*	£
	Digging out slurry from rut or hole in grassed area: removing and depositing arisings using wheelbarrows or the like on planked runs as directed: filling excavation with approved material to within 75 mm of surface: completing filling with approved topsoil, finishing level with surrounding surface after consolidation: raking: sowing grass seed: raking in: rolling: rut or hole	
E12	not exceeding 150 mm average deep	3.71
E13	150 to 300 mm average deep	5.39
E14	Scarifying surface of damaged grassed area: spreading approved topsoil to a consolidated average depth of 50 mm, including filling isolated hollows not exceeding 150 mm average deep: finishing level with surrounding surface: raking: sowing grass seed: raking in: rolling	2.02

F: Maintenance of Grassed Areas

GRASS CUTTING

GENERALLY

Specification

Notice: three days notice will be given for ordering the cutting of grass.

Cutters to all mowers: keep sharp and properly set to cut the sward cleanly and evenly. Set to the cutting height directed.

Flail type mowers and reapers: set to cut evenly and as close to the ground as directed.

Avoid damage to trees etc during current grass cutting operations. Replace at Contractor's expense all trees etc damaged by grass cutting operations.

Airfields and other large areas (excluding bird-strike deterrent areas): gang-mowing is the normal requirement for cutting grass but use multiple rotary type or flail type equipment if ordered.

Bird-strike deterrent areas: cut grass with multiple rotary type mowers minimum 3600 mm wide set to a cutting height of 150 mm. When ordered, bottom out.

Bottoming out grass on bird-strike deterrent areas:

a. use forage harvester or reaper with cutters set as low as possible;
b. clean out and remove arisings from grass cutting and naturally occurring thatch;
c. harrow and rake arisings into windrows and collect into trailers.

Note

Mowing out for line marking:
Pay for at the appropriate Rates *multiplied by 1.25.*

Rates for the following include

Generally:
For preliminary inspection of areas to be cut.

Cutting grass:
For cutting the whole of the area with the equipment ordered.

For cutting margins, corners, along wall and fence line bases and around obstructions using other suitable equipment if necessary, without additional payment.

For cutting on rough, sloping or uneven ground unless otherwise stated.

For cutting weeds and all growth of a non-woody nature.

For sweeping up arisings scattered on adjoining paths, roads, drives or the like and disposing.

For leaving arisings on the grass unless otherwise stated.

For disposing isolated items of obstructions eg stones, mole hills, rubbish or the like which might damage grass cutting equipment.

For cutting overgrowth of grass at edges of cultivated areas, fire breaks, hard surfaces, backs of kerbs, sand play-pits or the like with edging shears to clean straight or smooth curved lines on each occasion and disposing arisings.

For cutting grass on level areas and banks within secure areas used for storing explosives or flammable fuels by means of pneumatically or hydraulically driven equipment fitted with nylon line rotary cutters, where so ordered. Non-powered equipment rates will apply.

Re-forming edges:
For re-forming edges next to cultivated areas, buildings and steps including forming V-shaped channel not exceeding 25 mm wide at top next to kerbs and hard paved areas.

WORK EXECUTED USING EQUIPMENT MOUNTED ON OR TOWED BY TRACTOR

Item	*Hectare*	£
	Cutting grass	
F1	using multiple-gang mower with cylindrical cutters	4.81
F2	using three-unit gang mower with cylindrical cutters	11.96
	using multiple-rotary mower with vertical drive shaft and horizontally rotating bar or disc cutters: cutting width	
F3	not exceeding 2 m	8.19
F4	2 to 4 m	5.33
F5	exceeding 4 m	3.06
F6	Cutting grass, overgrowth or the like: using flail mower or reaper	14.43
F7	Bottoming out grass on bird-strike deterrent areas: removing and depositing arisings	67.60
	ADD for	
F8	burning arisings	3.90
F9	disposing arisings	13.65
	100 Square Metres	
	Cutting grass, overgrowth or the like: using tractor-mounted side-arm flail mower: in areas inaccessible to alternative machine: on surface	
F10	not exceeding 30° from horizontal	0.91
F11	30° to 50° from horizontal	1.89

WORK EXECUTED USING 'RIDE-ON' SELF-POWERED EQUIPMENT

Item	*100 Square Metres*	£
	Cutting grass	
F12	using multiple-cylinder mower fitted with cutting units mounted directly in such a manner as to permit one or more of the units to be disengaged and secured out of use for the purpose of working in confined or otherwise inoperable areas	0.39
F13	using multiple-rotary mower with horizontally rotating bar, disc or chain cutters	0.28
	ADD for using grass box/collector for	
F14	removing and depositing arisings	0.13
F15	disposing arisings	0.13

WORK EXECUTED USING PEDESTRIAN OPERATED SELF-POWERED EQUIPMENT

Item	*100 Square Metres*	£
	Cutting grass	
F16	using cylinder lawn mower fitted with not less than five cutting blades, front and rear rollers	0.65
	using rotary, flail or other suitable mower: on surface	
F17	not exceeding 30° from horizontal	0.52
	30° to 50° from horizontal	
F18	not exceeding 2 m high	1.57
F19	2 to 5 m high	2.09
F20	5 to 10 m high	2.61
F21	exceeding 10 m high	3.13
	exceeding 50° from horizontal	
F22	not exceeding 2 m high	2.09
F23	2 to 5 m high	2.61
F24	5 to 10 m high	3.13
F25	exceeding 10 m high	3.66
	ADD for using grass box for	
F26	removing and depositing arisings	0.13
F27	disposing arisings	0.13
F28	Cutting 'bents', flowering stalks or the like: using rotary mower on grassed area normally cut with a cylinder mower	0.39
	Cutting grass or light woody undergrowth: using trimmer with nylon cord or metal disc cutter: on surface	
F29	not exceeding 30° from horizontal	3.13
	30° to 50° from horizontal	
F30	not exceeding 2 m high	3.66
F31	2 to 5 m high	4.18
F32	5 to 10 m high	4.70
F33	exceeding 10 m high	5.22
	exceeding 50° from horizontal	
F34	not exceeding 2 m high	4.18
F35	2 to 5 m high	4.70
F36	5 to 10 m high	5.22
F37	exceeding 10 m high	5.75

WORK EXECUTED USING NON-POWERED EQUIPMENT

Item	*100 Square Metres*	£
	Cutting grass	
F38	using cylinder lawn mower fitted with not less than seven cutting blades, front and rear rollers: removing and depositing arisings	1.04
F39	ADD for disposing arisings	0.13
	on rough area: using scythe or similar implement: on surface	
F40	not exceeding 30° from the horizontal	4.70
	30° to 50° from horizontal	
F41	not exceeding 2 m high	5.22
F42	2 to 5 m high	5.75
F43	5 to 10 m high	6.27
F44	exceeding 10 m high	6.79
	exceeding 50° from horizontal	
F45	not exceeding 2 m high	5.75
F46	2 to 5 m high	6.27
F47	5 to 10 m high	6.79
F48	exceeding 10 m high	7.31
	100 Metres	
F49	Trimming or reforming edge of grassed area: using edging tool to straight or curved line: removing and depositing arisings	11.57
F50	ADD for disposing arisings	0.26
F51	Trimming back grass: any width: where encroaching on to surface of path: using edging tool to straight or curved line: removing and depositing arisings	18.80
F52	ADD for disposing arisings	0.30

CLEARING ARISINGS FROM GRASS CUTTING OR THE LIKE

Item	*Hectare*	£
F53	Removing and depositing	11.31
	ADD for	
F54	burning	3.90
F55	disposing	13.65

CLEARING ARISINGS FROM GRASS CUTTING OR THE LIKE—*continued*

Item	*100 Square Metres*	£
	Hand raking: removing and depositing: on surface	
F56	not exceeding 30° from horizontal	1.57
F57	30° to 50° from horizontal	2.09
F58	exceeding 50° from horizontal	2.61
	ADD for	
F59	burning	0.07
F60	disposing	0.13

PROTECTION OF GRASSED AREAS

Specification

Protective mesh: high density polyethylene with securing pegs. Obtain from an approved manufacturer.

a. For foot traffic: 20 mm square mesh with extra strengthening filaments at centre and edges, securing pegs 150 mm long.
b. For vehicle traffic: 27 mm round heavy duty mesh, securing pegs 280 mm long.

Lay and secure with pegs along all edges at maximum 1500 mm centres, drive pegs well into ground so that no projections will interfere with mowing.

Note

Cutting grassed areas prior to laying mesh: Pay for at the Rates in the 'Grass Cutting' Sub-section.

Rates for the following include

Generally:
For laps.

For cutting to shape or profile.

		1	2
		Foot traffic	Vehicle traffic
	Square Metre	£	£
	Protective mesh: on grassed area:		
F61	on surfaces not exceeding 30° from horizontal	3.07	3.88
	on surfaces 30° to 50° from horizontal		
F62	not exceeding 2 m high	3.13	3.93
F63	2 to 5 m high	3.17	3.98
F64	5 to 10 m high	3.23	4.04
F65	exceeding 10 m high	3.28	4.08

HARROWING

Item	Hectare	£
	Harrowing grassed area: removing and depositing arisings: using	
F66	chain or light flexible spiked harrow	9.10
F67	drag harrow	18.20
F68	ADD for disposing arisings	3.90

SCARIFYING

Item	Hectare	£
	Scarifying grassed area: removing and depositing arisings: using	
F69	equipment mounted on or towed by tractor	20.80
F70	ADD for disposing arisings	3.90
	100 Square Metres	
F71	pedestrian operated self-powered equipment	0.88
F72	hand implement	2.09
F73	ADD to Items F71 and F72 for disposing arisings	0.20

ROLLING

Item	Hectare	£
	Rolling grassed area: using equipment towed by tractor at a speed not exceeding 5 km/h: once over: using	
F74	smooth three-gang roller	8.06
F75	smooth single-section roller	14.17
	100 Square Metres	
	Rolling small grassed area: around building, sports pitch, lawn or the like: using equipment at a speed not exceeding 5 km/h: once over: using	
F76	'ride-on' self-powered roller	0.60
F77	pedestrian operated self-powered roller	0.85
F78	hand roller	1.76

TURF AERATION

Item	*Hectare*	£
	Aerating grassed area: using	
F79	turf aerating equipment towed by tractor: to effect a minimum penetration of 100 mm	19.50
F80	tractor-mounted equipment with power driven tines: to effect a minimum penetration of 300 mm at 100 mm centres	305.50
	100 Square Metres	
F81	pedestrian operated self-powered solid or slitting tine turf aerating equipment to effect a minimum penetration of 100 mm	0.78
F82	pedestrian operated self-powered hollow tine turf aerating equipment: to effect a minimum penetration of 100 mm: sweeping up: removing and depositing arisings	2.54
F83	hollow tine hand implement: to effect a minimum penetration of 100 mm and spaced 150 mm apart: sweeping up: removing and depositing arisings	6.50
F84	hand fork: to effect a minimum penetration of 100 mm and spaced 150 mm apart ...	5.46
F85	ADD to Items F82 and F83 for disposing arisings	0.13

LEAF CLEARANCE

	Hectare	£
	Clearing grassed area of leaves and other extraneous debris: removing and depositing arisings: using	
F86	equipment mounted on or towed by tractor	17.16
	ADD for	
F87	burning arisings	3.90
F88	disposing arisings	13.65
	100 Square Metres	
F89	pedestrian operated self-powered equipment	0.61
F90	hand implement	1.04
	ADD to Items F89 and F90 for	
F91	burning arisings	0.07
F92	disposing arisings	0.13

LITTER CLEARANCE

Item		£
	Hectare	
F93	Picking up and collecting litter: from grassed area: disposing	10.85
	100 Square Metres	
F94	Picking up and collecting litter: from isolated grassed area not exceeding 1000 m^2: disposing	0.39

BRUSHING

		£
	100 Square Metres	
	Brushing grassed sports areas	
F95	using drag brush or net towed by tractor	0.20
F96	hand brushing or switching	0.52

FOREIGN OBJECT DAMAGE CONTROL

Definition

Foreign objects: anything lying on cultivated, grassed or hard surfaces which might damage vehicle or aircraft tyres or be ingested into aircraft engines.

Rates for the following include

Generally:

For preliminary inspection.

For removing isolated foreign objects.

For removing foreign objects from any surface.

		£
	Hectare	
F97	Picking up by hand and collecting foreign objects: disposing: where specifically ordered	12.54

G: Fertilizers, Pesticides and Top Dressing

GENERALLY

Specification

Chemicals: use only materials on the Ministry of Agriculture Approved Lists.

Application of chemicals: apply chemicals in accordance with the manufacturer's instructions. Operatives handling fertilizers and pesticides are required to be of certified competence in accordance with the provisions of the Food and Environment Protection Act 1985.

Clean equipment after use with each different type of material. Pesticides must be applied with equipment used for fertilizers.

Notes

Generally:
The Contractor shall make good at his own expense any damage caused as a result of his negligence in the use of chemicals.

Cultivation: when ordered, pay for at the appropriate Rates in the 'Preparation of Land' Section.

Supplying materials:
Pay for separately.

Rates for the following include

Generally:
For any necessary mixing with water.

Spreading and applying:
For spreading and applying at the coverage rates ordered.

FERTILIZERS

Specification

Distribution: except on lawns, shrub beds or other small areas, distribute by mechanical spreader. On lawns, shrub beds and other small areas, mark out the area to be dressed to ensure even distribution and distribute by mechanical hand spreader or by hand.

Item	*Hectare*	£
	Spreading	
	by vehicle-mounted mechanical spreader: over ground	
G1	granular or pelleted fertilizer—*per 250 kilogrammes per hectare*	10.66
G2	lime—*per tonne per hectare*	6.83

Item		£
	100 Square Metres	
	Spreading	
G3	by mechanical hand spreader or by hand: over lawn: granular or pelleted fertilizer or lawn dressing—*per kilogramme per 100 m²*	0.33
	Square Metre	
G4	by hand over shrub bed or the like: organic, granular or powdered fertilizer—*per 25 grammes per m²*	0.07

PESTICIDES (INCLUDING WEEDKILLERS) ETC

Specification

Application by spraying: do not spray when rain is expected or in windy conditions, which could cause drifting that would damage nearby vegetation. Do not use volatile pesticides in hot weather when vapour drift might damage susceptible plants and greenhouse crops. Take every precaution to ensure that spraying is confined to the area to be treated.

Wear required protective clothing when handling concentrates, washing off splashes from the skin immediately. Wash hands before meals and after work.

Keep containers tightly closed and in a safe place.

Rates for the following include

Applying by spraying:
For wettable powder or liquid chemicals.

Item		£
	Hectare	
	Applying by	
G5	vehicle-mounted or trailer boom spraying equipment: selective weedkiller, growth regulator or pesticide	15.21
	100 Square Metres	
	knapsack or hand sprayer	
G6	over grassed area or hardstanding: selective or total weedkiller, growth regulator, mosskiller or fungicide	3.64
	Square Metre	
G7	over plants in shrub bed or the like (measure ground area): selective weedkiller, fungicide or pesticide	0.07
G8	on sides and top of hedge (measure girth of hedge): growth regulator, fungicide or pesticide	0.07
	100 Metres	
G9	on construction or other joint in paving, at fence line, kerb edge or at base of building: strip not exceeding 300 mm wide: total weedkiller	1.76
	Hectare	
	Spreading	
	granular or pelleted pesticide: over grassed area	
G10	by vehicle-mounted mechanical spreader	10.66

Item	*100 Square Metres*	£
	Spreading	
	granular or pelleted pesticide: over grassed area	
G11	by mechanical hand spreader	0.33
	granular selective or total weedkiller: by mechanical hand spreader	
G12	over ground	0.33
	100 Metres	
G13	at fence line, kerb edge or at base of building: strip not exceeding 300 mm wide ...	0.20

TOP DRESSING

Item	*Hectare*	£
	Spreading	
	by vehicle-mounted mechanical spreader—*per tonne per hectare*	
	over ground	
G14	sand, ash or the like	8.19
G15	loam, manure, peat or sewage sludge	10.92
	over sports pitch or the like	
G16	sand, ash or the like	10.92
G17	loam or peat	13.65
	100 Square Metres	
	by hand: over lawn—*per 10 kilogrammes per 100 m^2*	
G18	sand, ash or the like	0.91
G19	loam, peat or compost	0.98

H: Trees, Shrubs and Other Plants

GENERALLY

Scope

Work in this Section comprises the planting and maintenance of trees, hedge plants, shrubs including roses, herbaceous and annual bedding plants and bulbs.

Specification

Nursery stock: comply with BS 3936.

Container-grown plants:
a. Do not remove from containers until planting areas have been prepared.
b. Ensure minimum damage to roots.
c. Remove and dispose 'bio-degradable' containers.

Handle trees and shrubs in accordance with the Joint Council of Landscape Industries 'Code of Practice for Plant Handling'.

Stakes: treated softwood: 'full length' or 'shortened' as ordered.

Ties and buffer pads: adjustable reinforced rubber ties and buffer pads fixed with galvanised nails.

Backfilling: if so directed remove and deposit excavated material and backfill with topsoil from elsewhere on the site.

Transport all materials over grassed areas using wheelbarrows on planked runs.

Notes

Supplying trees, shrubs, plants, bulbs, etc:
Pay for separately.

Supplying fertilizers and soil ameliorants:
Pay for separately.

Cultivation:
When so ordered, pay for at the appropriate Rates in the 'Preparation of Land' Section.

Backfilling using topsoil from elsewhere on the site:
Pay for at the appropriate Rates in the 'Soft Landscaping' Section.

Rates for the following include

Planting generally:
For planting any item as ordered.

For watering-in.

Stakes, ties and buffer pads:
For supplying and fixing.

PLANTING TREES, SHRUBS, HEDGES AND OTHER PLANTS

Planting in pits and trenches

Excavate pits and trenches sufficiently wide and deep to accommodate the full spread of roots and to the following minimum sizes:

a. Forestry transplant and whip:	500 × 500 × 500 mm deep
b. Feathered:	1000 × 1000 × 500 mm deep
c. Standard and heavy standard:	1250 × 1250 × 750 mm deep
d. Extra heavy standard:	1500 × 1500 × 900 mm deep
e. Hedge plants— single row:	500 × 300 mm deep
double row:	750 × 300 mm deep

Plant in pits or trenches, backfilling with selected excavated material to level of surrounding ground and carefully working it among the roots; firm around the plants so that they are securely anchored and with the collars at surface level.

Planting in pits and trenches—*continued*

In grassland place excavated soil on plastic sheet to prevent damage to the turf.

Add fertilizer and/or soil ameliorants and mix into the planting soil and base of excavation as directed.

Fork over bottom of excavation to a depth of 225 mm.

Drive stakes firmly into position after excavating and before planting; set on the prevailing windward side of the plant.

Prune back damaged roots to sound tissue.

Prune crowns of trees at time of planting where directed.

Secure trees (other than forestry transplants and feathered trees) to stakes with approved reinforced rubber ties nailed to the stake.

Surplus arisings from planting: remove and deposit.

After planting, rake surface of soil, remove and deposit arisings and leave tidy.

Planting in prepared beds or containers etc

Set out in the order and to the spacings and depths directed.

Plant by excavating holes large enough to accommodate the full spread of the roots and with the best side of each plant to the front. Backfill planting holes with selected excavated material or compost and firm around the collars of the plants.

Grouped annual bedding plants: plant edges in lines or curves as appropriate and fill in the centre by planting in a random manner.

Plant bulbs taking account of type and variety.

Shallowly fork over or rake surface of planted border as appropriate, remove and deposit arisings and leave tidy.

Planting bulbs or corms in grassed areas

Scatter to achieve random drifts over the area specified.

Plant by carefully cutting and lifting turf and excavating hole not exceeding 150 mm deep using a trowel or auger. Replace turf and firm down.

Item	*Metre*	1 Single row £	2 Double row £
	Excavating trench: planting hedge plants: stakes and ties: transplants		
H1	not exceeding 600 mm high	1.30	2.34
H2	600 to 1200 mm high	1.63	2.67

Item	*Per 100*	£
	Planting herbaceous or annual bedding plants, bulbs, tuberous plants or corms in	
H3	prepared beds	6.76
H4	grassed areas	8.24
H5	containers, window boxes, etc	8.50

Item	*Each*	£
	Planting in prepared bed	
H6	herbaceous plant where dead or diseased plant removed	0.15
H7	shrub	0.33
H8	ADD to Items H6 and H7 where in containers, window boxes, etc	0.41
H9	forestry transplant or whip	0.39
H10	feathered tree	0.65
	Excavating pit: planting	
H11	forestry transplant or whip	2.60
H12	feathered tree	4.03

Item	Each	1 Single stake £	2 Double stake £
	Excavating pit: planting tree: stakes, ties and buffer pads		
H13	standard	17.40	20.25
H14	heavy standard	26.50	33.00
H15	extra heavy standard	—	47.30

TREE GUARDS, STAKES AND TIES, ETC

Item	Each	£
H16	Adjusting existing tree tie	0.13
H17	Taking up single or double tree stake and ties: removing and disposing	0.23
	Taking down tree guard and stake: setting aside for re-use or disposing	
H18	plastics tree shelter or spiral rabbit guard	0.59
H19	galvanised wire or plastics mesh guard	0.65
	Refixing tree guard: any type: with new galvanised wire staples	
H20	re-using stake previously set aside	1.17
H21	providing new stake	2.50
H22	Taking off and disposing broken or decayed tie: new tie and buffer pad	2.05
	New stake, ties and buffer pads	
H23	single stake	3.10
H24	double stake	5.10
	Rabbit guard: plastics spiral: wrapping around trunk	
H25	450 mm high	0.58
H26	600 mm high	0.69
H27	750 mm high	0.79
	Tree guard: semi-rigid slotted polypropylene: not exceeding 75 mm diameter: fitting around trunk: base pushed slightly into ground	
H28	150 mm high	0.44
H29	300 mm high	0.69
H30	600 mm high	1.14
H31	1200 mm high	2.09
H32	1800 mm high	2.74

TREE GUARDS, STAKES AND TIES, ETC

Item	Each	1	2	3
		Diameter		
		200 mm	250 mm	300 mm
		£	£	£
	Tree guard: circular: welded mesh: 12 gauge wire: 75 × 25 mm mesh: galvanized: supplied in two pre-shaped halves: fixing together around tree with fixing clips: adjusting height where necessary to avoid obstructing branches			
H33	525 mm high: two clips	4.12	6.96	8.34
H34	825 mm high: two clips	6.13	9.20	11.21
H35	1200 mm high: four clips	9.87	12.11	14.58
H36	1800 mm high: four clips	11.36	14.81	18.09

Item		£
	Tree shelter: translucent corrugated plastics: 75 × 75 mm: spot welded joints: double thickness top: fixing with one piece plastic non-slip ratchet fixing clips: stake	
H37	600 mm high	1.53
H38	1200 mm high	1.87
H39	1500 mm high	2.13
	Mulching mat: cutting and fitting to profile around tree and stake(s)	
H40	polythene: 600 × 600 mm	0.39
H41	standard bitumen felt: 500 × 500 mm	0.63

PRUNING SHRUBS

Specification

Generally: use only skilled labour.

Tools: keep sharp and properly set. Do not use mechanical hedge cutters or the like.

Make all cuts cleanly without tearing.

Prune all shrubs so as to maintain their shape and balance in order to produce the best decorative effect.

Cut out all dead, damaged and weak wood, tie in branches of climbing and wall plants.

Arisings: remove and deposit or dispose as directed and leave tidy.

Prune:

a. *Spring or early summer flowering deciduous shrubs* immediately after flowering, by pruning out all stems on which flowers have been borne, and thin out young shoots.

b. *Summer or autumn flowering deciduous shrubs* as soon as growth begins in the spring, cutting back previous year's growth to within two or three buds of the older wood.

c. *Deciduous shrubs grown for foliage or coloured stem effect* by cutting back close to ground level early in March.

d. *Evergreen shrubs* in May, early June, or September, removing dead wood and any weak or unsightly growth that spoils the natural habit of the plant.

e. *Hybrid tea and floribunda roses* in March by cutting out dead and weak growth; select strong stems to form balanced framework and prune these back to four to six buds from old wood, selecting outward facing buds.

f. *Rose stems* in Autumn by approximately one third to prevent wind rock.

g. *Climbing roses* in March by tying stems to form a balanced framework, prune sideshoots from main stem to two to four buds.

h. *Rambling roses* in July or August by removing stems that have borne flowers, space out and tie in current year's stems to form an evenly balanced framework.

j. *Shrubs massed in borders* by thinning out old wood and flower stems, and judicious pruning to reduce height and density by approximately 25%.

k. *Ground cover shrubs* such as Hypericum calycinum by cutting close to ground level in Spring.

l. *Heathers* by clipping tips of shoots that have flowered in order to maintain a compact habit.

Dead head floribunda or hybrid tea roses by cutting stems, where flowers have faded, back to within four or five buds of the previous year's wood.

Removal of excess growth, dead or diseased climbing plants or shrubs from face of building: carefully remove from walls, under tiles or slates, around windows, doors, fascia boards, down pipes, gutters, etc, including removing leaves and debris from gutters and re-tying or re-wiring in as necessary.

Note

The Rates for pruning do not include for topiary work.

Rates for the following include

Generally:
For the use of steps, ladders, trestles, or tower scaffolding or the like.

For removing and depositing or disposing arisings.

Item		£
	Square Metre	
H42	Trimming ground cover planting	0.42
H43	Pruning massed shrub border (measure ground area)	0.52
	Each—per plant	
	Cutting off dead heads	
H44	bush or standard rose	0.31
H45	climbing rose	1.55
	Pruning	
H46	bush or standard rose	1.04
H47	climbing rose or rambling rose: tying in as required	6.26
	ornamental shrub: height before pruning	
H48	not exceeding 1 m	1.55
H49	1 to 2 m	2.08
H50	exceeding 2 m	2.62
H51	When pruning has not been executed during the previous two years, multiply the Rates for Items H48 to H50 by 1.50.	
	Removing excess growth etc from face of building etc: height before pruning	
H52	not exceeding 2 m	6.56
H53	2 to 4 m	9.75
H54	4 to 6 m	16.08
H55	6 to 8 m	63.76
H56	8 to 10 m	102.56

PRUNING SHRUBS

Item	*Each—per shrub or tree*	£
	Removing epicormic growth from base of shrub or trunk and base of tree: any height: any diameter: number of growths	
H57	not exceeding 10	0.78
H58	10 to 20	1.82

TREE SURGERY

Scope

Work in this Section is applicable to mature trees only.

Specification

Carry out in accordance with BS 3998 and current Forestry Safety Council guides, using only skilled labour.

Tools: keep sharp and properly set.

Make all cuts cleanly without tearing.

Branches severed from main trunk: leave a projection of 50 mm proud of the branch source and 'bark collar'.

Lower cut timber to the ground using ropes.

Avoid damage to adjacent trees or property.

Stack cordwood and felled timber (where to be retained) in neat piles or as directed.

Method of measurement

Diameter of branch:
Measure at the final cut point.

Pollarding:
Measure only branches exceeding 50 mm diameter.

Height above ground level:

a. Removing isolated branch or part branch: Measure to the final cut point.
b. Pollarding: Measure to the highest cut point.

Rates for the following include

Generally:
For the use of hand saws or hand held mechanical chain saws.

For removing branches of any length.

For cutting timber into manageable lengths and stacking.

Pollarding:
For removing all growths not exceeding 50 mm diameter.

		1	2	3
		Diameter of branch		
		not exceeding 100 mm	100 to 300 mm	300 to 600 mm
	Each	£	£	£
	Removing isolated damaged or diseased branch or part branch: removing and depositing arisings: height above ground level			
H59	not exceeding 5 m	11.90	15.60	19.30
H60	5 to 10 m	14.35	18.05	21.90
H61	10 to 15 m	16.85	20.55	24.25
H62	15 to 20 m	19.30	23.00	26.70
	ADD for			
H63	burning arisings	0.65	0.90	0.95
H64	disposing arisings	1.70	2.16	2.60

Item	Each—per tree	1	2	3	4
		Height above ground level		ADD for	
		not exceeding 5 m	5 to 10 m	burning arisings	disposing arisings
		£	£	£	£
H65	Pollarding: branches or part branches: any diameter exceeding 50 mm: re-shaping tree: removing and depositing arisings: not exceeding 10 branches	50.00	55.00	5.95	12.90
H66	ADD *for each additional branch*	3.50	3.60	0.90	2.16

J: Beds, Borders, Planters Etc

GENERAL MAINTENANCE

Specification

Lifting spring bulbs: carefully lift bulbs, clean off, treat with fungicide, store in sand filled boxes or cold frames to ripen during the summer.

Lifting tubers and corms: cut down plant, carefully lift, clean off and treat with fungicide and store in a frost proof shelter.

Lifting annual bedding plants: remove by hand.

Lifting established herbaceous plants: cut down, carefully lift plants, propagate by division, discarding the central woody crown. Label and heel-in offsets of divided plants in temporary location during the cultivation and preparation of beds and borders.

Temporary staking and tying in: provide softwood stakes or canes and twine to herbaceous plants as directed.

Hand weeding beds, borders and planters, etc: carefully hand weed in a way which will not damage plants, remove dead plants, spent flowers, inflorescences, discoloured leaves and stems, remove litter and leaves and erase footprints from beds and borders with a hand fork.

Notes

Supplying compost, mulch, processed bark and soil ameliorants:
Pay for separately.

Edging of beds and borders with edging tool:
Pay for at the Rates in the 'Maintenance of Grassed Areas' Section.

Application of fertilizers and pesticides:
Pay for at the Rates in the 'Fertilizers, Pesticides and Top Dressing' Section.

Rates for the following include

Generally:
For work to flower and shrub beds and borders, planters and the like and bases around trees.

For working carefully to avoid damage to stems, branches and roots of trees, shrubs and plants.

For removing and depositing or disposing arisings.

Temporary staking:
For additional tying in to herbaceous plants during the growing season.

Digging, hoeing and raking:
For grading cultivated surfaces to an even convex profile lightly consolidated.

Weeding, digging, hoeing, raking and cultivating:
For collecting weeds, plants, leaves, litter, stones and debris at the time of execution of the work, removing and depositing and leaving area tidy (Pay for leaf, litter and debris clearance at other times, under Rates J30 to J32).

Item	*Per 100*	£
J1	Dead heading bulbs: in temporary or permanent planting stations	1.00
	Lifting	
J2	bulbs	9.55
J3	tubers or corms	8.40
J4	bedding plants	3.00
J5	established herbaceous plants	62.68

Item		£
	Each	
J6	Temporary staking and tying in herbaceous plant	1.96
	Cutting down spent growth of herbaceous plant	
J7	unstaked	0.15
J8	staked: not exceeding 4 stakes per plant: removing stakes and putting into store ...	0.25
	100 Square Metres	
J9	Hand weeding	12.54
J10	Hand digging with fork: not exceeding 150 mm deep: breaking down lumps: leaving surface with a medium tilth	25.07
J11	Hand digging with fork or spade to an average depth of 230 mm: breaking down lumps: leaving surface with a medium tilth	28.20
J12	ADD to Items J10 and J11 for incorporating soil ameliorants	7.50
J13	Hand hoeing: not exceeding 50 mm deep: leaving surface with a medium tilth	18.80
J14	Hand raking to remove stones etc: breaking down lumps: leaving surface with a fine tilth prior to planting	4.70
	Each	
	Hand weeding: planter, window box, etc: any shape: surface area of filling material	
J15	not exceeding 0.25 m²	0.52
J16	0.25 to 0.50 m²	1.04
J17	0.50 to 0.75 m²	1.57
J18	0.75 to 1.00 m²	2.09
J19	exceeding 1.00 m²	2.61
	Hand cultivating: planter, window box, etc: not exceeding 150 mm deep: any shape: surface area of filling material	
J20	not exceeding 0.25 m²	1.04
J21	0.25 to 0.50 m²	1.57
J22	0.50 to 0.75 m²	2.09
J23	0.75 to 1.00 m²	2.61
J24	exceeding 1.00 m²	4.17
	Circular bed: approximately 750 mm diameter: around base of tree in grassed area	
J25	maintaining by hand hoeing or digging	0.91
J26	forming by hand digging	1.43
J27	ADD to Items J25 and J26 for incorporating soil ameliorants	0.50
	Square Metre	
	Spreading compost, mulch or processed bark to a depth of 75 mm	
J28	on shrub bed	0.20
	Each	
J29	on circular bed approximately 750 mm diameter: around base of isolated tree	0.13

Item	*100 Square Metres*	£
	Clearing cultivated area of leaves, litter and other extraneous debris: using hand implement	
J30	removing and depositing arisings	1.56
	ADD for	
J31	burning arisings	0.07
J32	disposing arisings	0.13

K: Hedging

GENERALLY

Specification

Generally:
Use only skilled labour.

Tools: keep sharp and properly set.

Use lines and canes to obtain even height and line of hedge where directed.

Collect, remove and deposit all arisings and leave tidy.

CUTTING FIELD AND ORNAMENTAL HEDGES

Specification

Generally:
Make cuts cleanly without tearing.

Field hedges: trim with hand tools, hand held mechanical trimmers, chain saws or tractor-mounted hedge cutting equipment as directed.

Ornamental hedges: trim with hand tools or hand held mechanical trimmers. Do not use flail cutters.

Reducing width or height of overgrown hedges: cut back to an even line or height;

a. Ornamental hedges; using hand tools, hand held mechanical trimmers or chain saws as directed. Do not use flail cutters.
b. Field hedges; using hand tools, hand held mechanical trimmers, chain saws or tractor-mounted hedge cutting equipment as directed.

Hedge bottoms: cut down all weeds, clean out base to outer profile of the cut hedge.

Definitions

Trimming sides and top of field hedge:
Cutting not exceeding 2 years' growth since last cut.

Trimming sides and top of ornamental hedge:
Cutting not exceeding 1 year's growth since last cut.

Cutting to reduce width or height of overgrown hedge:
Cutting back field hedge exceeding 2 years' growth since last cut.

Cutting back ornamental hedge exceeding 1 years' growth since last cut.

Method of measurement

Trimming sides and top of hedge:
Measure the girth by the length after the work has been executed.

Cutting to reduce width or height of overgrown hedge:
Measure the average depth of cut from the original side or top to the finished side or top.

Measure the area after the work has been executed.

Item	Square Metre	1 Using hand tool or hand held mechanical tools £	2 Using tractor-mounted hedge cutting equipment £	3 ADD for burning arisings £	4 ADD for disposing arisings £
	Trimming sides and top of hedge				
	field hedge				
K1	not exceeding 2 m high	0.15	0.09	0.05	0.10
K2	2 to 4 m high	0.25	0.12	0.05	0.10
	ornamental hedge				
K3	not exceeding 2 m high	0.10	—	0.05	0.10
K4	2 to 4 m high	0.15	—	0.05	0.10

Item		1	2	3	4	5	6
		Using hand tools or hand held mechanical tools			Using tractor-mounted hedge cutting equipment		
		Average depth of cut					
		not exceeding 300 mm	300 to 600 mm	600 to 900 mm	not exceeding 300 mm	300 to 600 mm	600 to 900 mm
		£	£	£	£	£	£
	Cutting to reduce						
	width of overgrown hedge						
	field hedge—*per side*						
K5	not exceeding 2 m high	0.73	1.04	1.35	0.12	0.23	0.34
K6	2 to 4 m high	0.94	1.25	1.56	0.18	0.29	0.40
K7	4 to 6 m high	1.15	1.46	1.67	0.24	0.34	0.46
	ADD for						
K8	burning arisings	0.05	0.10	0.15	0.05	0.10	0.15
K9	disposing arisings	0.15	0.20	0.25	0.15	0.20	0.25
	ornamental hedge—*per side*						
K10	not exceeding 2 m high	0.52	0.83	1.15	—	—	—
K11	2 to 4 m high	0.73	1.04	1.35	—	—	—
K12	4 to 6 m high	0.94	1.25	1.56	—	—	—
	ADD for						
K13	burning arisings	0.05	0.10	0.15	—	—	—
K14	disposing arisings	0.15	0.20	0.25	—	—	—
	height of overgrown hedge						
	field hedge						
K15	not exceeding 2 m high	0.94	1.25	1.56	0.18	0.29	0.40
K16	2 to 4 m high	1.15	1.46	1.77	0.23	0.34	0.46
K17	4 to 6 m high	1.35	1.67	1.98	0.29	0.40	0.51

Item		1	2	3	4	5	6
		Using hand tools or hand held mechanical tools			Using tractor-mounted hedge cutting equipment		
		Average depth of cut					
		not exceeding 300 mm	300 to 600 mm	600 to 900 mm	not exceeding 300 mm	300 to 600 mm	600 to 900 mm
		£	£	£	£	£	£
	Cutting to reduce—*continued*						
	height of overgrown hedge—*continued*						
	field hedge—*continued*						
	ADD for						
K18	burning arisings	0.05	0.10	0.15	0.05	0.10	0.15
K19	disposing arisings	0.15	0.20	0.25	0.15	0.20	0.25
	ornamental hedge						
K20	not exceeding 2 m high	0.73	1.04	1.35	—	—	—
K21	2 to 4 m high	0.94	1.25	1.56	—	—	—
K22	4 to 6 m high	1.15	1.46	1.77	—	—	—
	ADD for						
K23	burning arisings	0.05	0.10	0.15	—	—	—
K24	disposing arisings	0.15	0.20	0.25	—	—	—

CUTTING AND LAYING FIELD HEDGES

Specification

Cut and lay hedges:

a. Lay the branches to an angle slightly above the horizontal and make the cuts in the stems at such an angle that they will shed water.
b. Make stakes and binders from material cut out of the hedge.
c. Drive stakes into the centre of the hedgerow line at 1 m centres and intertwine the branches in such a way as to form a strong stock-proof barrier with no gaps.
d. Neatly finish the laid hedge with binders woven between the tops of the stakes.

Cut away branches and twigs in the hedgerow that are not required for laying, clean out base of hedge and leave tidy.

Hedgerow trees: leave standing in the hedgerow those trees selected and marked by the SO.

Rates for the following include

Generally:
For providing any additional stakes that may be required.

	Metre	1	2	3
			ADD for burning arisings	ADD for disposing arisings
		£	£	£
	Cutting and laying field hedge: any sectional area: cutting all growth not exceeding 600 mm girth: depositing arisings: average width			
K25	not exceeding 2 m	7.09	0.15	0.91
K26	2 to 4 m	10.10	0.25	1.22

L: Watering

Definitions

Hand held watering equipment: Hosepipe not exceeding 25 mm bore with spray nozzle for use on small grass or amenity planting areas where the SO decides that the use of unattended equipment is not practicable.

Perforated or trickle hose: For use in shrub beds and herbaceous borders. Lay without kinks.

Single portable rotating or oscillating sprinkler unit: For use on small grass or amenity planting areas.

Portable sprayline unit: Oscillating or rain-gun type: for use on large areas of grass and for hard porous recreational areas. Use in groups of three or more.

Watering cans: Of adequate capacity and fitted with a rose.

Note

The number of hours of watering: as ordered.

Rates for the following include

Generally:
For supplying stand-pipes, hosepipes, fittings, approved spray nozzles, sprinklers and spraylines.

For connecting to water supply and dismantling on completion.

For moving equipment around the site.

For applications either prior to or after planting.

Sprinklers and spraylines:
For erecting and re-siting where necessary.

Watering from bowser:
For collecting water and transporting any distance by towed bowser of any capacity.

Item	*Hour*	£
	Watering	
	evenly over an area within 100 m of standpipe: using	
L1	hand held watering equipment	10.08
L2	perforated or trickle hose	1.50
L3	single portable rotating or oscillating sprinkler unit	1.82
L4	ADD *for each additional or subsequent unit*	0.39
L5	group of three portable sprayline units	2.28
L6	ADD *for each additional or subsequent unit*	0.46
L7	evenly over an area within 25 m of water bowser: using hand held watering equipment	13.00
L8	planters, window boxes, pots and hanging baskets using either hand held watering equipment from mains supply or bowser, or using watering cans	15.00

M: Maintenance of Domestic Gardens

Scope

The work in this Section comprises the maintenance of enclosed domestic gardens and typically includes grass cutting, clearing weeds, maintenance of beds and borders, hedge trimming etc or other work as ordered.

Note

Where a number of similar domestic gardens are to be maintained under the same order, the Contractor and the SO will agree on the work to be carried out in a typical garden.

Pay for all similar gardens as for the typical garden.

Item		
	Maintenance of domestic gardens	
	pay for at the appropriate Rates in other Sections multiplied by the following factors	
	garden	
M1	not exceeding 250 m^2	multiply by 1.70
M2	250 to 500 m^2	multiply by 1.60
M3	500 to 1000 m^2	multiply by 1.50
M4	exceeding 1000 m^2	no adjustment

N: Cemetery Work

GENERALLY

The Contractor's attention is drawn to the sensitive nature of the work and he must ensure noise levels are kept to a minimum. Under no circumstances will the use of radios, audio equipment, etc be permitted.

Ensure no damage is caused to monumental masonry, trees, shrubs, paths and grassed areas during the execution of the works.

Make good any damage caused at the Contractor's expense.

GRAVE DIGGING

Specification

Notice: normally three to five days will be given prior to commencement of the works.

Turf: cut and lift turf and stack in neat piles adjacent to the work ready for re-laying.

Excavate grave 100 mm wider and longer than the size of the coffin.

Erect shuttering around grave area to protect adjacent graves.

Supply and place in position grave shields, landing boards and jacks to stabilise grave sides.

On completion of excavation supply and lay artificial grass over the excavated soil.

On completion of funeral service:

a. Carefully backfill and pack evenly.
b. Dispose of surplus excavated material.
c. Re-lay turf to marry in with existing ground levels.
d. Leave the area clean and tidy on completion.

Rates for the following include

Generally:
For executing work by hand.

For using skilled labour and supervision.

For providing shuttering, grave shields, landing boards, jacks and artificial grass and removing on completion.

Item	*Each—per grave*	£
	Stripping turf, excavating grave, backfilling, removing and disposing surplus excavated material: re-laying turf	
N1	single grave 1.95 m deep	148.00
N2	double grave 2.55 m deep	178.00

MAINTENANCE OF GRAVES

Specification

Erecting head stone: collect from store, carefully load and transport to graveside. Excavate for base, set and surround base with concrete (20 N/mm^2: 20 mm aggregate), ensure that it is set true and level and remove and dispose of surplus excavated material and reinstate turf.

General maintenance to individual graves: cut grass or weed areas by hand and prune any shrubs, bushes or perennial flowers as necessary.

Wash down and carefully clean monumental masonry and surround.

Dispose of all arisings and leave area tidy.

Notes

Headstones:
Supplied by others.

Supplying cleaning materials:
Pay for separately.

Cutting general grassed areas within cemetery:
Pay for at the Rates in the 'Maintenance of Grassed Areas' Section.

Rates for the following include

Generally:
For any double handling of monumental masonry from transport vehicle to graveside.

Item		£
	Each—per head stone	
N3	Erecting head stone	46.50
	Each—per grave	
N4	General maintenance to grave	7.42
	Square Metre	
N5	Washing down and cleaning monumental masonry and surround	1.56

P: Sports Areas

GRASSED SPORTS AREAS

LINE MARKING

Specification

Marking out of sports areas, setting out and placing of equipment: conform to the current recommendations of the governing body of the relevant sport unless otherwise directed.

Marking materials: apply approved marking materials so that lines remain clearly marked for a minimum of seven days. Add no weed killers, creosote or the like to the marking out material.

Lines: straight or to curves at the radii required.

Note

Mowing out for line marking:
Pay for at the appropriate Rates in the 'Maintenance of Grassed Areas' Section.

Rates for the following include

Generally:
For supplying marking material.

Initial marking:
For measuring and setting out.

Item	*Each*	1 Initial marking £	2 Over-marking £
	Marking		
P1	volleyball pitch	22.10	6.90
P2	netball pitch	33.10	10.25
P3	hockey pitch	50.70	13.65
P4	football pitch	63.70	16.40
P5	five-a-side football pitch	44.10	13.65
P6	rugby pitch	87.10	26.00
P7	rounders pitch	33.80	9.50
P8	softball pitch	42.25	12.35
P9	baseball pitch	40.95	12.35
P10	American football pitch	162.50	46.80
P11	cricket boundary	24.70	11.05
P12	400 m running track not exceeding 8 lanes	218.40	71.50
P13	shot putt area	16.25	5.45
P14	javelin area	18.20	6.90
P15	hammer throw or discus area	16.25	5.45
P16	high jump fan	20.80	6.90
P17	long jump approach	12.15	3.80
P18	tennis court	32.50	9.50

REPAIRS

Note

Supplying grass seed:
Pay for separately.

Rates for the following include

Filling depressions or holes:
For supplying approved filling material.

Item	*Each—per pitch*	£
	Inspecting sports surface: replacing divots or filling small depressions: firming ground: re-seeding as necessary	
P19	hockey pitch	15.00
P20	football pitch	19.50
P21	five-a-side football pitch	5.20
P22	rugby pitch	22.10
P23	softball pitch	19.50
P24	baseball pitch	19.50
P25	American football pitch	35.75
P26	shot putt area	6.50
P27	javelin area	6.50
P28	hammer throw or discus area	6.50
P29	tennis court	5.20
P30	Filling holes for goal posts (any game): firming ground: re-seeding as necessary	5.20

HARD SPORTS AREAS

Note

Provision, maintenance and repairs and marking out of Non-Porous Surfaces:
Pay for at the Rates in the 'Hard Landscaping' Section.

POROUS WATER-BOUND SURFACES

Specification

Shale or crushed rock:
Obtain from an approved manufacturer.

Lay 50 mm thick using hand implements, 'ride-on' self-powered or pedestrian operated self-powered equipment.

Compact with a 2/3 tonne smooth dead-weight roller, spray with water and roll again to achieve approved degree of compaction and to produce an approved playing surface.

Notes

Excavating, filling and surface treatment of formation:
Pay for at the Rates in the 'Hard Landscaping' Section.

Supplying plastic marking tape and fixing pins:
Pay for separately.

Method of measurement

New shale or crushed rock surfacing:
Measure area in contact with base.

POROUS WATER-BOUND SURFACES—*continued*

Make no deduction for voids not exceeding 0.50 m^2.

Measure the compacted thickness.

Rates for the following include

Setting out lines:
For temporary guide lines.

For checking dimensions/layouts.

Fixing or refixing marking tape:
For laying to straight or curved lines with neatly formed joints.

For fixing with pins.

For rolling flush to surrounding levels.

Brushing:
For removing extraneous material from marking tapes.

Item	100 Square Metres	£
P31	New shale or crushed rock surfacing: 52 mm thick: rolling: watering: re-rolling	394.16
P32	Scarifying to a depth of 25 mm: disposing arisings: scarifying formation: spreading shale or crushed rock surfacing material 25 mm thick: grading with reverse edge of a 'Trulute' or other approved implement: watering: dragging mat over surface: brushing: rolling to produce an approved playing surface	207.87
P33	Scarifying to a depth not exceeding 25 mm: removing and disposing weeds or the like: levelling using the cutting edge of a 'Trulute' or other approved implement: watering: dragging mat over surface: brushing: rolling to produce an approved playing surface ...	9.41
P34	Sweeping up debris: removing and disposing arisings	3.14
P35	Levelling out footprints or the like: watering: dragging mat over surface: brushing: rolling to produce an approved playing surface	4.70
	Metre	
P36	Taking up marking tape fixed with pins: setting aside for re-use	0.10
P37	Refixing displaced marking tape	0.10
P38	Fixing marking tape	0.21
P39	Setting out lines to sports areas: fixing marking tape	0.31

CRICKET PITCHES

GENERALLY

Specification

All operations must be executed in the Sequence directed and in an approved manner by skilled labour.

Chemicals:
Use only chemicals on the Ministry of Agriculture Approved Lists.

Note

Supplying grass seed, fertilizers and weedkillers:
Pay for separately.

Rates for the following include

Generally:
For supplying approved filling materials and loam.

Pitches:
For pitches size 23 × 3 m.

Patches:
For patches of any size.

Tables:
For tables size 30 × 30 m.

PREPARING GRASSED CRICKET PITCH

Item	*Each—per pitch*	£
P40	Cutting grass using fine cut mower set to a cutting height of 4 mm: raking: brushing and repeating cutting in opposite direction: disposing arisings: rolling using hand roller weighing not less than 150 kg as conditions require to prepare pitch to an approved degree of firmness: marking out creases	32.50
P41	Commencing four days before day of match, selecting position of pitch parallel to line of corner pegs: scarifying using either hand implements or with two passes of pedestrian operated self-powered equipment set to operate above soil profile: brushing up: disposing arisings: cutting grass using fine cut mower set to a cutting height of 4 mm: brushing and repeating cutting in opposite direction: disposing arisings: watering to provide compressible surface by allowing water to soak into surface: rolling using hand roller or pedestrian operated self-powered roller weighing not more than 1500 kg to an approved standard of firmness: repeating brushing, cutting and rolling daily during the preparation. On the morning of the day of the match, cutting grass to a height of 4 mm: disposing arisings: rolling using hand roller or pedestrian operated self-powered roller weighing not more than 500 kg: marking out creases	74.10

PREPARING SYNTHETIC SURFACED CRICKET PITCH

Note

Adjacent grass:
Cut a strip 3 m wide adjacent to the pitch using a pedestrian operated self-powered mower fitted with a grass box and trim edge at junction with pitch.

Pay for at the appropriate Rates in the 'Maintenance of Grassed Areas' Section.

Item	*Each—per pitch*	£
P42	Commencing on the day before the match, sweeping surface of pitch: disposing arisings. On the morning of the day of the match, rolling using hand roller or pedestrian operated self-powered roller to an approved standard of firmness: re-marking creases with external quality emulsion paint	8.80
P43	Watering surface of pitch using hand held hosepipe fitted with coarse rose, without overlapping on to adjacent grass: watering clay in stump boxes	7.50

RENOVATING GRASSED CRICKET PITCH

Item	*Each—per pitch*	£
P44	Sweeping up torn turf and debris: disposing arisings: aerating pitch to a depth of 100 mm using hand fork or pedestrian operated self-powered equipment: brushing or raking to raise nap of turf: forking over hollows: correcting levels using screened sterilized loam: compacting by treading: raking surface to form seed bed as necessary: sowing cricket table mixture grass seed at a rate of 50 g per m^2: raking in: rolling seeded area using hand roller: watering	20.50

RENOVATING SYNTHETIC SURFACED CRICKET PITCH

Item	*Each—per pitch*	£
P45	Removing synthetic mat, underlay and shock pads: scarifying hard porous water-bound base using the cutting edge of a 'Trulute' or other approved implement: filling depressions with hard porous water-bound material of similar type and quality to existing: watering: raking and rolling to produce an approved level surface: refixing underlay and shock pads, excavating base as necessary beneath the shock pads to produce a true and level base for the mat: refixing mat with 100 mm galvanised nails or nylon pins, pulled taut to provide an approved playing surface	161.70
	Each—per patch	
P46	Repairing minor damage to synthetic mat by spreading contact adhesive over damage, building up in layers until flush with surrounding area: sprinkling rovings of mat material over adhesive whilst still tacky: touching up with external quality emulsion paint to match existing	9.10
P47	Repairing major damage to synthetic mat by cutting out rectangular patch containing the damage: applying 100 mm wide plastic adhesive tape to underside around edge of hole, leaving 50 mm wide strip exposed: patching by accurately fitting matching material, firmly fixed at edges to adhesive tape: sealing joint with contact adhesive: sprinkling rovings of mat material over adhesive whilst tacky: touching up with external quality emulsion paint to match existing: removing and disposing arisings	32.50

RENOVATING GRASSED CRICKET TABLE

Item	*Each—per table*	£
P48	Scarifying with two passes using hand implement or pedestrian operated self-powered equipment set to penetrate 10 mm into the soil: sweeping up, removing and disposing arisings: aerating using hand fork or pedestrian operated self-powered solid tine aerating equipment to effect a minimum penetration of 100 mm spaced 150 mm apart: applying fine turf autumn fertilizer at a rate of 50 g per m^2: applying wormkiller in accordance with the manufacturer's instructions: top dressing with not exceeding 4 tonnes of screened sterilised heavy loam, filling depressions, raking and brushing in to attain smooth surface: sowing cricket table mixture grass seed at a rate of 10 g per m^2: raking in: rolling seeded area using hand roller: watering	546.00

BOWLING GREENS

GENERALLY

Specification

Execute all operations in the sequence directed using skilled labour. Ensure no lift or damage is caused during maintenance operations.

Cutters to all mowers: keep sharp and properly set to cut the sward cleanly and evenly. Set to the height directed.

Cutting greens: use a fine turf cylinder lawn mower fitted with not less than ten blades, front and rear rollers and grass collection box.

Cutting perimeter banks: use suitable equipment and carry out at time of cutting the green.

Scarifying to control thatch: use approved pedestrian operated self-powered equipment. Sweep, brush up or box off all arisings. Leave a clean tidy surface.

Aeration: use approved pedestrian operated self-powered equipment to effect a minimum penetration of 100 mm. Irrigation must fully penetrate the root zone, avoid surface wetting.

GENERALLY—*continued*

Specification—*continued*

Top dressing: ensure even distribution of material, using a lute, working from the undressed areas. Integrate dressing into the surface and/or aeration voids, brush or drag mat upon completion until completely worked in. Use planked wheelbarrow runs to protect the greens.

Turf in repairs: of approved quality

a. Cut and remove turf from either a nursery bed, an appointed place on the green or obtain from an approved supplier.
b. Do not strip or lay turf when weather is exceptionally dry, when surfaces are waterlogged or during frost or snow.
c. Re-lay turf within seven days of stripping. Ensure that the programme of stripping is co-ordinated with that of re-laying.
d. Ensure all repairs evenly fit without gaps and are level with adjoining areas. Adjust any deviation from specified levels by lifting, raking out or infilling with approved filling material and, rolling.
e. Where turf has been removed from nursery area, make good by returning worn turf or dressing and seeding with selected grass seed of an approved quality.
f. Where turf has been removed from an appointed area on the green make good with turf from either nursery area, imported turf or with selected grass seed of an approved quality.
g. Use planked wheelbarrow runs to protect the greens.

Grass seeds: named cultivars of certified EEC 'Blue Label' quality and within the supplier's time limit. Mixtures of seeds as ordered. Uncertified seeds will not be accepted.

a. Sow seeds only when weather and soil conditions are approved.
b. Sow seeds at the coverage rates directed evenly by hand, rake in and roll with light hand roller.

Chemicals: use only chemicals on the Ministry of Agriculture Approved Lists.

Watering: maintain adequate moisture in the greens at all times during maintenance operations.

Notes

Cutting perimeter banks:
When ordered, pay for at the appropriate Rates in the 'Maintenance of Grassed Areas' Section.

Fertilizing:
When ordered, pay for at the appropriate Rates in the 'Fertilizers, Pesticides and Top Dressing' Section.

Supplying grass seed, turf, fertilizers, top dressings or compost mix:
Pay for separately.

Rates for the following include

Generally:
For bowling greens size 38.41 × 38.41 m (42 × 42 yds).

For preliminary inspection of the greens to be worked on.

For checking of measurements, removing strings from store and fixing where ordered prior to the commencement of the playing season.

For providing planked timber barrow runs including moving and adjusting as necessary.

For collecting and depositing all arisings from the maintenance operations, including leaves, litter etc.

For watering.

Raising levels:
For supplying approved filling materials.

Cutting grass:
For cutting straight or diagonal swards.

For cutting margins and into corners.

For sweeping up arisings scattered on adjoining paths, paved areas, perimeter ditch, drainage channels and gulleys and removing and depositing.

Turf generally:
For temporary stacking.

For transporting.

Turf cut from nursery area:
For making good using worn turf from green or re-seeding.

Turf cut from appointed area on green:
For making good using imported turf or re-seeding.

AUTUMN MAINTENANCE

Item	*Each—per green*	£
P49	Switching dew from green first thing each morning and keeping grass cut to 5 mm high during maintenance operations: removing and placing in store all strings and greens equipment: taking up and removing stones and filling from perimeter ditch and placing in an approved storage area: scarifying the green with the blades set so as not to penetrate the soil but to lift procumbent growth and thatch layer by 4 to 6 successive passes, each diagonally opposed to the last: overseeding with specified cultivars at the rates directed to any thin or worn areas, firstly ensuring an adequate key for grass seed by lightly pricking with a hand fork and raking	267.03
	Each—per green—per occasion	
	Aerating using	
P50	spike roller	14.84
P51	solid tines	44.51
P52	vertically power driven hollow tines in single pass to effect maximum penetration at 50 mm centres	57.70
	Cubic Metre	
P53	Top dressing green with an approved compost mix or straight dressing as directed ...	44.51

WINTER MAINTENANCE

Note

This work is to commence as soon as all top dressing material has weathered into surface of green.

	Each—per green	£
P54	Switching or brushing dew from green first thing each morning, removing any litter or debris on and around the green and checking for any disease to the turf: as growth dictates keeping the green topped to 8 mm: *over a 4 week period*	148.35
	Square Metre	
	Cutting out and removing worn turf and laying	
P55	imported turf	2.25
P56	turf cut from nursery area or appointed area on the green	9.67
P57	Rectifying levels using a straight edge to determine the extent of the depression: evenly spreading approved dressing to low areas: lightly raising level using a border/hand fork so as not to disrupt or damage the surface or root zone: working dressing into aerated voids: applying no more material than can be integrated fully without surface damage or smothering turf	7.42
P58	Raising depressed levels to edge of green, using a border fork inserted to depth of root zone and gently easing out compaction without causing undue damage to surface or root system	1.85

WINTER MAINTENANCE—*continued*

Item	*Square Metre*	£
P59	Raising depressed levels to green using a straight edge and levelling equipment to determine the extent of the depression: cutting, lifting and rolling back turf sufficiently to allow corrective levelling: lightly forking surface beneath turf: applying an approved pre-turfing fertilizer: integrating and raising levels with filling material consolidated by heeling and treading: re-laying turf adequately firming and working from planks: top dressing turf with approved top dressing material, spreading with a lute and well brushing in	11.13

SPRING MAINTENANCE

Item	*Each—per green*	£
P60	Switching or brushing dew from green first thing each morning, and removing any litter or debris on or around the green: commencing re-firming the surface by rolling with a 'Tru-level' roller or equivalent or a fine turf mower with blades disengaged passed slowly over the surface: as weather and ground conditions improve increasing the weight of the roller to 100 to 150 kg and rolling in different directions to firm the green without compaction: repeating as required up to opening of the green: topping with fine turf mower gradually reducing the height of cut to 5 mm: lightly scarifying the green across the two diagonals: spike rolling: overseeding any persistent weak areas with approved cultivars: lightly top dressing with approved material 0.5 to 1 m^3 as required, spreading with a lute and well brushing in: removing all debris: cleaning gullies: washing and replacing stone or filling to perimeter ditch: washing and cleaning area where stones were stored: removing all greens equipment from store as directed and setting in position ready for play: *over a 6 to 8 week period*	778.84

SUMMER MAINTENANCE (Rink and Match Management)

Item	*Each—per green*	£
P61	Switching or brushing dew from green first thing each morning, and removing any litter and debris on or around the green: brushing and keep cutting to a height of 5 mm on the diagonal, the frequency and timing dependent upon weather conditions and match preparation: lightly rolling once with a 'Tru-level' smooth roller or equivalent: removing and re-laying lines during cutting operations, adjusting positions to minimise wear to greens or position of rinks all in conjunction with the match or game schedule: *over a 1 week period*	148.35
P62	Aerating green with spike roller or spike slitter	14.84

GOLF COURSES

GENERALLY

Notes

Generally:
Rates in other Sections apply to work on golf courses where Rates are not given in this Sub-Section.

Supplying grass seed:
Pay for separately.

Application of fertilizers, top dressing etc:
Pay for at the appropriate Rates in the 'Fertilizers, Pesticides and Top Dressing' Section.

Rates for the following include

Generally:
For preliminary inspection.

For removing and depositing arisings.

Filling depressions and holes:
For supplying approved filling material.

FAIRWAYS AND TEES

Item	*Hectare*	£
P63	Replacing divots or filling depressions: firming ground: re-seeding as necessary	18.00

PUTTING GREENS

Notes

Supplying cups and flag sticks:
Pay for separately.

'Ride-on' self powered equipment:
Power unit to be fitted with flotation tyres.

Rates for the following include

Cutting grass:
For the use of specialist fine turf mowers.

Item	*100 Square Metres*	£
	Cutting grass with mower fitted with not less than ten blades, front and rear rollers and grass collection box: using	
P64	pedestrian operated self-powered equipment	0.80
P65	'ride-on' self-powered equipment	0.50
	Aerating using	
P66	spike roll	1.06
P67	solid or slit tines	3.02
P68	vertically power driven hollow tines	3.19
P69	Rolling: using roller of 500 kg spread over three integrated rollers	1.90
P70	Hand brushing or switching	0.52
P71	Repairing pitch marks: using approved repair tool	0.85
	Each	
P72	Cutting hole: using purpose made hole cutter: trimming perimeter: inserting cup and flag stick	1.50
	Filling hole: removing flag stick and cup: consolidating to level of surrounding area: re-seeding as necessary	
P73	with 'plug' cut from new hole	0.40
P74	with approved topsoil and turf cut from nursery area or appointed area on the green ...	1.05

BUNKERS

Specification

Sand filling:
Quantity and quality as ordered.

Rates for the following include

Filling depressions:
For supplying approved filling materials.

Item	*100 Square Metres*	£
P75	Loosening sand: removing and disposing large stones, debris and weeds: filling small depressions: raking over to give an even surface	5.10
	Cubic Metre	
P76	Excavating by hand to remove old sand filling	9.00
	Disposing excavated material	
P77	off site	9.50
P78	on site: transporting a distance not exceeding 1 km and depositing	5.60
P79	ADD *for each additional 0.25 km of transporting distance*	0.65
P80	Sand filling to bunker: raking over to give an even surface	22.00

SUNDRIES

Specification

Sand filling to jump landing area: of type and quality ordered.

Notes

Supplying sand filling:
Pay for separately.

Supplying goal post sockets:
Pay for separately.

Rates for the following include

Goal posts:
For fitting nets, net supports, back boards, protectors etc, as appropriate.

Dismantling:
For taking down, cleaning, loading, transporting and placing in store.

Erecting:
For removing from store, loading, transporting, cleaning out post sockets and erecting in position.

		1	2
		Dismantling	Erecting
	Each—per pitch or court	£	£
P81	Rounders posts	7.00	7.00
P82	Hockey goal posts	19.50	19.50
P83	Football goal posts	19.50	19.50
P84	Five-a-side football goal posts	13.65	13.65
P85	Rugby goal posts	28.60	28.60
P86	American football goal posts	28.60	28.60
P87	Volleyball net and posts	13.00	14.00
P88	Tennis net and posts	13.00	15.00
P89	Cricket square fencing	15.60	20.80
P90	Cricket sight screens	28.60	28.60

Item	*Each—per pitch or court*	£
P91	Digging holes for, and bedding in ground, goal post sockets: any game: making good ground … … … … … … … … … … … … … … …	25.10
P92	Removing from store marker posts and placing in position: tightening and adjusting goal nets: subsequently taking up marker posts and returning to store: slackening off goal nets: any game … … … … … … … … … … … … … …	6.85
	Each	
P93	Digging out disused or damaged goal post sockets: any game: making good ground: removing and disposing arisings … … … … … … … … … … …	6.85
	Square Metre	
	Jump landing area	
P94	loosening sand: raking over to give a level, even surface … … … … … …	0.47
P95	excavating sand 300 to 450 mm deep: brushing out: refilling with sand: raking over to give a level, even surface: removing and depositing arisings … … … … …	2.49

Q: Playgrounds

PLAYGROUND EQUIPMENT: FIXING ONLY

Specification

Generally:
Assemble, erect and test strictly in accordance with the manufacturer's instructions.

Note

Ground-fixed items:
Heights stated are the heights above ground.

Rates for the following include

Ground-fixed items:
For excavating holes for supports, bases, etc and disposing of arisings.

For breaking through existing hard surfacings.

For setting into ground at depth recommended by the manufacturer or as ordered.

For setting horizontally, vertically or raking as appropriate or as ordered.

For filling holes for supports, bases, etc with concrete (20N/mm^2: 20 mm aggregate) to the full depth.

Item	Each			1	2
				Height	
				2400 mm	3000 mm
				£	£
	Swing: any type				
	Number of seats	*Number of ground fixing points*			
Q1	1	2	... ...	17.75	19.36
Q2	1	4	... ...	30.66	32.28
Q3	2	4	... ...	33.89	35.50
Q4	3	4	... ...	37.11	38.73
Q5	4	6	... ...	50.03	51.64
Q6	5	6	... ...	53.25	54.86
Q7	6	6	... ...	56.48	58.08

Item		£
Q8	Swing area safety barrier: 1250 mm wide: 900 mm high: two ground fixing points ...	13.00

Slide: steps, deck and handrails: six ground fixing points

Item	*Overall length*	*Overall height*	*Deck height*		£
Q9	3350 mm	1600 mm	1000 mm	... ...	66.15
Q10	4150 mm	2400 mm	1500 mm	... ...	72.60

SAFETY SURFACING

Note

For other surfacing suitable for playgrounds see 'Hard Landscaping' Section.

GRANULATED RUBBER SAFETY TILES

Specification

Tiles:
Slip resistant, solid plain backed or solid rubber buffer cone backed.

Obtain from an approved manufacturer and lay in accordance with their instructions.

Primer/adhesive:
Obtain from the tile manufacturer.

Rates for the following include

Generally:
For cleaning off surplus adhesive from face of tiling.

For all necessary cutting.

Fair joint to flush edge of existing paving:
For preparing edge of existing paving.

Item		1	2	3	4
		Plain backed tiles			Cone backed tiles
		Bevelled edged		Square edged	
		Overall thickness			
		20 mm	50 mm	85 mm	50 mm
	Square Metre	£	£	£	£
	Surfacing: solid: level and to falls only: tile size				
Q11	500 × 500 mm	—	—	104.60	—
Q12	600 × 600 mm	47.85	75.60	—	—
Q13	750 × 750 mm	40.75	72.10	—	76.45
Q14	1000 × 1000 mm	—	—	91.25	—
	ADD where				
Q15	to falls and crossfalls and to slopes not exceeding 15° from horizontal	1.25	1.25	1.25	1.25
	in repairs				
Q16	not exceeding 1 m²	7.70	10.35	13.15	10.65
Q17	1 to 5 m²	3.85	5.20	6.56	5.33
	Metre				
	Tapered edge tile				
Q18	100 mm wide	7.45	—	—	—
Q19	200 mm wide	—	9.90	—	—
Q20	Fair joint to flush edge of existing paving	1.24	1.90	2.55	1.90
Q21	Straight kerb edge tiles: 100 mm wide	—	—	—	10.45

GRANULATED RUBBER SAFETY TILES—*continued*

		1	2	3	4
		Plain backed tiles			Cone backed tiles
		Bevelled edged		Square edged	
		Overall thickness			
		20 mm	50 mm	85 mm	50 mm
Item	*Each*	£	£	£	£
Q22	Extra over Item Q21 for angle	—	—	—	9.75
Q23	Cutting and fitting around obstructions not exceeding 0.30 m girth	0.60	0.95	1.35	0.95
Q24	ADD *for each additional 0.30 m of girth*	0.37	0.57	0.75	0.57

R: Hard Landscaping

EXCAVATING AND FILLING

GENERALLY

Specification

Safety: ensure the safety of all personnel working in and around excavations.

Protection: protect excavations against frost.

Water disposal:

a. Keep excavations free of water at all times.

b. Remove water so that it does not enter construction work.

c. Where pumping is necessary form sumps clear of excavations for permanent work.

Obstructions: report to the SO details of any underground obstructions.

Excavations taken too wide or too deep: backfill as ordered at the Contractor's own expense.

Foundation bottoms:

a. Excavate the last 150 mm of trenches immediately prior to laying concrete.

b. Inform the SO and obtain his instructions if natural bearing bottom cannot be found at the prescribed depths because solid rock is encountered, the ground is made up or is otherwise unsuitable for building upon.

c. Obtain approval before laying concrete.

Definitions

Ground level: Ground, stripped or reduced level.

Rock: A material which in the opinion of the SO can be removed only by means of wedges, special plant or explosives.

Ground water: Excludes spring or running water.

Notes

Excavation below ground water level:
If ground water is encountered in the course of excavation, the water level will be established by the SO before pumping is commenced (in tidal conditions this will be the average of the mean high and low levels), and the level so established will be taken as the water level throughout the period of the execution of the order notwithstanding any changes.

Depths stated:
Relate to ground level.

Site clearance:
Pay for at the appropriate Rates in the 'Clearance' Section.

Method of measurement

Excavating and disposal:
Measure the void to be occupied by, or vertically above the permanent work. Make no allowance for variations in bulk or for extra space for earthwork support.

Working space:
Measure additional excavation up to a maximum of 600 mm from faces of formwork, rendering, tanking or protective walls which are less than 600 mm from the face of the excavation.

Do not adjust if more or less space is actually required.

Rates for the following include

Excavating, disposal and filling:
For multiple handling unless specifically ordered.

Curved earthwork support:
For any extra costs of curved excavation.

EXCAVATING

Note

Excavating pipe trenches and manhole/soakaway pits:
Pay for at the appropriate Rates in the 'Drainage' Section.

Rates for the following include

Excavating:
For excavating by hand or machine any material encountered (including hardcore) except where otherwise stated.

For keeping the excavations free of surface water.

Excavating below ground water level:
For keeping excavations free of ground water.

Item	*Square Metre*	£
R1	Topsoil for preservation: 150 mm average depth	0.33
R2	ADD or DEDUCT *for each 25 mm variation in depth*	0.04

Item	*Cubic Metre*	1	2	3
		Maximum depth not exceeding		
		0.25 m	1.00 m	2.00 m
		£	£	£
R3	To reduce levels	2.48	2.41	2.50
R4	Pit	7.66	6.96	7.99
R5	Trench not exceeding 0.30 m wide	9.32	9.27	9.54
R6	Trench exceeding 0.30 m wide	6.70	6.79	7.27

Item		£
R7	Extra over excavation irrespective of depth for excavating below ground water level	2.09
	Extra over excavation irrespective of depth for breaking out	
R8	rock	23.25
R9	concrete	25.47
R10	reinforced concrete	38.51
R11	brickwork, blockwork or stonework	13.81
	Square Metre	
R12	concrete paving—*per 25 mm of thickness*	0.55
R13	reinforced concrete paving—*per 25 mm of thickness*	0.76
R14	concrete or stone flag paving: not exceeding 75 mm thick	0.67
R15	brick paving: not exceeding 125 mm thick	0.80
R16	stone sett or cobble paving: not exceeding 150 mm thick	1.21
R17	coated macadam or asphalt paving—*per 25 mm of thickness*	0.44

R18 Where hand excavation is specifically ordered, multiply the foregoing Rates by 2.00

EXCAVATING—*continued*

Item	*Metre*	£
	Extra over excavation irrespective of depth for excavating	
R19	next existing service or group of services	6.56
	Each	
R20	around existing service or group of services crossing excavation	19.75

EARTHWORK SUPPORT

Definitions

Unstable ground: Running silt, running sand, loose gravel or the like.

Earthwork support next to roadway or existing building: Earthwork support which, in the opinion of the SO, is required to protect any adjacent roadway or building from movement or damage.

Method of measurement

Earthwork support:
Measure the full depth to all vertical and sloping earthwork faces exceeding 45% from horizontal, whether or not support is required, except to faces not exceeding 0.25 m high.

Earthwork support below ground water level or in unstable ground:
Measure from the commencing level of the excavation to the full depth.

Distances between opposing faces:
Classify with adjoining work at intersections, corners or ends of trenches or the like.

Rates for the following include

Generally:
For providing everything to uphold the sides of excavation by whatever means necessary including sheet steel piling unless this is ordered as a specific design requirement.

		1	2
		Maximum depth not exceeding	
		1.00 m	2.00 m
	Square Metre	£	£
	To face of excavation: distance between opposing faces		
R21	not exceeding 2.00 m	3.02	3.50
R22	2.00 to 4.00 m	3.22	3.93
R23	exceeding 4.00 m	5.62	7.26
	ADD where		
R24	curved	1.79	2.04
R25	below ground water level	5.36	5.90
R26	in unstable ground	4.18	4.53
R27	next to roadway	3.37	4.01
R28	next to existing building	8.08	3.23

DISPOSAL

Rates for the following include

Generally:
For any type of excavated or broken out material.

Item	*Cubic Metre*	£
	Excavated material	
R29	off site ...	9.30
R30	on site: transporting a distance not exceeding 25 m and depositing ...	4.25
R31	ADD *for each additional 50 m of transported distance* ...	0.84

FILLING

Specification

Earth filling: approved readily compacted subsoil, free from harmful contaminants or vegetable matter and suitable for the location.

Granular filling: gravel, sandy soil or other approved material free from fines, clay or other harmful matter.

Spread filling in layers; compact and consolidate each layer before spreading the next.

Hardcore: hard stone, concrete, coarse gravel, sound slag or hard broken brick, free from rubbish or other deleterious matter, capable of passing in every direction a ring of diameter not greater than two thirds thickness of bed, subject to a maximum diameter of 150 mm and graded so that when compacted, filling is dense and without voids.

Spread hardcore in layers and compact:

a. with mechanical plant until all movement in the hardcore ceases;
b. until all voids are full and surface is smooth and even.

Approval: backfill only with approval.

Rates for the following include

Filling:
For compacting in layers not exceeding 150 mm thick.

Hardcore obtained from the excavations or demolitions:
For selecting for re-use and breaking to required sizes.

		1	2	3	4	5
		Selected excavated material arising from excavations on site	Imported material		Hardcore	
			Earth	Granular	Obtained from the excavations or demolitions	Imported
	Cubic Metre	£	£	£	£	£
	Filling to excavation					
R32	not exceeding 0.25 m average thick ...	8.61	14.43	24.17	11.20	18.69
R33	exceeding 0.25 m average thick ...	7.18	12.99	22.74	9.33	16.82
	Filling to make up levels					
R34	not exceeding 0.25 m average thick ...	9.70	15.52	25.27	12.62	20.11
R35	exceeding 0.25 m average thick ...	8.09	13.91	23.66	10.51	17.99

SURFACE TREATMENTS

Item	Square Metre	£
	Levelling or grading to falls and slopes not exceeding 15° from horizontal: compacting	
R36	ground or earth or granular filling	0.65
R37	hardcore filling	0.98
R38	bottom of excavation	0.30
R39	Blinding surface of hardcore with approved fine material	1.11
R40	Trimming sloping surface exceeding 15° from horizontal	1.05
R41	Trimming bottom or side of excavation in rock to falls, slopes or cambers	12.36

POWER PUMPING

Note

Generally:
When not in connection with removing surface water or ground water encountered during excavations, working time only (ie the actual hours of pump running time) will be paid for the use of pumps as ordered.

Rates for the following include

Generally:
For bringing to and removing from the site.

For moving about the site as required.

For hoses.

For operating.

For disposal of water.

For attendance.

Item	Hour	£
	Single diaphragm pump	
R42	75 mm	2.26
R43	100 mm	3.20
	Double diaphragm pump	
R44	75 mm	2.63
R45	100 mm	3.94
	Self-priming centrifugal pump	
R46	50 mm	1.26
R47	75 mm	1.78
R48	100 mm	3.52

IN SITU CONCRETE

SPECIFICATION

Generally

British Standards: concrete is to comply with BS 5328 and BS 8110, unless otherwise specified.

Constituent materials

Cement:

a. Ordinary and rapid-hardening Portland cement to BS 12 and manufactured by a BSI Registered Firm.

b. Sulphate-resisting Portland cement to BS 4027 and manufactured by a BSI Registered Firm.

c. Do not use pulverised fuel ash, ground granulated blast furnace slag and/or any other cementitous materials unless ordered.

Aggregates: to BS 882. Do not use marine aggregates or aggregates which contain chlorides.

Water: clean and uncontaminated. Obtain approval for other than mains supply.

Curing Compounds: of proprietary manufacture and

a. approved before use;
b. having a minimum efficiency of 90% when tested to BSI DD 147;
c. containing a fugitive dye.

Mix Proportions:

a. Ready mixed concrete: in compliance with BS 5328, Tables 1 and 2 appropriate to grade of concrete required with medium workability;
b. Concrete, site mixed to BS 5328: as shown in the following Table:

Grade N/mm^2	Mix by Weight		Mix by Volume		Aggregate Nominal Size (mm)	Acceptable Range of Slump (mm)
10	Cement Fine aggregate Coarse aggregate	50 kg 170 kg 280 kg	Cement Fine aggregate Coarse aggregate	50 kg 0.10 m^3 0.20 m^3	40	50–100
20	Cement Fine aggregate Coarse aggregate	50 kg 100 kg 200 kg	Cement Fine aggregate Coarse aggregate	50 kg 0.06 m^3 0.14 m^3	20	25–75
30	Cement Fine aggregate Coarse aggregate	50 kg 80 kg 150 kg	Not applicable		20	25–75

NOTE: Small deviations from the amounts of aggregates shown in the Table may be permitted by the SO where necessary to produce satisfactory concrete but the total weight or volume of aggregate given must not be exceeded.

Site mixed concrete

Handling and storage of constituent materials:

a. Cement: obtain in sealed bags or containers, store in dry enclosed conditions on a raised platform separating different types of cement. Use in order of delivery.
b. Aggregates: store on a hard, clean base which permits free drainage keeping different types and sizes separate. Protect from frost and contamination by deleterious materials.

Batching and mixing: comply with Section 13 of BS 5328. Do not use frozen or frost covered materials. Ensure workability of concrete is such that:

a. it can be readily worked into corners and angles of forms and around reinforcement;
b. constituent materials do not segregate and free water does not collect at the surface during placing.

Ready-mixed concrete

Supplier: obtain ready mixed concrete from an approved supplier.

Information to be provided to supplier: provide ready mixed concrete supplier with the following information:

a. concrete grade;
b. type of cement;
c. mix proportions;
d. embargo on use of other cementitious materials and marine aggregates;
e. acceptable slump;
f. requirement of compliance with BS 5328.

SPECIFICATION—*continued*

Placing

Avoidance of contamination: avoid contamination, segregation or loss of ingredients, by cleaning transporting equipment immediately after use or whenever cement or aggregate is changed. Remove free water.

Plasticity: place concrete whilst it is still sufficiently plastic for full compaction to take place. Record time and date of all concrete pours.

Compaction: compact concrete thoroughly around reinforcement, duct formers, inserts and into corners of formwork. Ensure full compaction and amalgamation with previous batches. Do not allow segregation.

Construction joints: lightly roughen entire face to expose coarse aggregate. Thoroughly wire brush to remove all loose material. Ensure face is clean and damp before fresh concrete is placed.

Cold weather working: do not place concrete when air temperature is below 6°C:
a. do not place or cast against frozen surfaces;
b. maintain temperature of placed concrete at not less than 7°C for at least five days after placing by approved method;
c. do not use water spraying or wet coverings when freezing temperatures are likely;
d. cover concrete surfaces with an insulating material when temperature reaches 10°C and is falling.

Frost damage: remove and replace concrete damaged by frost.

Curing

Curing period: not less than 7 days unless otherwise ordered.

Curing method: as ordered and either:
a. waterproof sheeting kept in close contact; or
b. absorbent material kept damp; or
c. an approved curing compound.

PATHS AND PAVED AREAS—ADDITIONAL REQUIREMENTS

Assemble and fix side forms accurately to required lines and levels. Secure in position with locking plates if necessary to ensure rigidity and obviate any movement during concrete laying and compacting.

Additives: do not use without the permission of the SO.

Underlay: lap sheets 150 mm at all joints. Lay on sub-base before placing concrete.

Laying and compacting:
a. Place and compact concrete continuously to prescribed joints. Spread and strike off with surcharge sufficient to obtain required compacted thickness.
b. Use compaction equipment of approved mechanical beam pattern with poker vibrators at edges and ends of slabs. Avoid contact between poker vibrators and fabric reinforcement. Obtain full slab depth compaction, uniform density and strength with appropriate number of passes of compaction equipment.
c. To ensure that proper compaction is being achieved, cut core samples from slabs, when required by the SO.
d. Concreting stopped between joints to be finished off vertically as a construction joint.

Finish smooth with an approved scraping straightedge immediately after completing compaction to produce a dense, even textured surface free from laitence and excessive water. Check surface with 3000 mm straightedge and immediately make good irregularities exceeding 6 mm. Draw a broom with medium coarse fibres transversely across the still-wet surface.

Other finishes: as ordered.

CONCRETE

Notes

Concrete generally:
Make no additional payment where approval is given to the use of Portland rapid-hardening cement of ready-mixed concrete. The additional Rates for Portland rapid-hardening cement shall be allowed only when used on the specific instructions of the SO.

Pouring concrete against faces of excavation:
Where the Contractor is permitted to pour concrete against faces of excavation, make no extra payment should he select to use formwork.

Method of measurement

Concrete volume:
Measure net but make no deduction for:
a. reinforcement;
b. voids not exceeding 0.05 m^3 in volume.

Rates for the following include

Concrete generally:
For Prescribed or Designed Mixes.

For ordinary Portland cement unless otherwise stated.

For medium or high workability.

For hand compacting or mechanically vibrating.

For curing.

For protecting concrete by any means when poured on or against earth or unblinded hardcore.

Bed, path or paving:
For laying in bays where ordered.

Item	*Cubic Metric*	1	2	3	4	5	6
		Plain			Reinforced		
		20 N/mm^2: 22 mm aggregate					
		Thickness					
		not exceeding 150 mm	150 to 450 mm	exceeding 450 mm	not exceeding 150 mm	150 to 450 mm	exceeding 450 mm
		£	£	£	£	£	£
R49	Bed, path or paving	88.01	82.53	79.38	91.19	85.71	82.55
R50	Wall	96.63	90.84	87.01	108.60	99.79	93.86

Item		1	2
		Plain	Reinforced
		20 N/mm^2 : 20 mm agg	
		£	£
R51	Foundation	84.01	89.48
R52	Isolated foundation	87.33	91.92
R53	Step or upstand	98.57	112.69

CONCRETE—*continued*

Item	*Cubic Metre*	£
	ADD to the foregoing Rates for bed, path or paving where sloping	
R54	not exceeding 15° from horizontal	3.76
R55	exceeding 15° from horizontal	7.51

ADJUSTMENTS TO FOREGOING RATES FOR OTHER MIXES AND CEMENTS

		1	2	3
		Plain or Reinforced		
		Ordinary cement	Rapid-hardening cement	Sulphate-resisting cement
	Cubic Metre	£	£	£
	ADJUST for			
	10 N/mm²			
R56	40 mm aggregate	− 7.79	− 6.61	− 4.74
R57	20 mm aggregate	− 5.04	− 3.78	− 1.63
	20 N/mm²			
R58	40 mm aggregate	− 2.05	− 0.50	+ 1.96
R59	20 mm aggregate	Nil	+ 1.67	+ 4.35
R60	10 mm aggregate	+ 3.78	+ 5.69	+ 8.77
	30 N/mm²			
R61	20 mm aggregate	+ 6.45	+ 8.53	+ 11.88
R62	10 mm aggregate	+ 11.87	+ 14.20	+ 18.11

FORMWORK

Specification

Materials for temporary formwork: wood, plywood, metal or plastic sheet material of sufficient strength, rigidity and durability.

Release agents: neat oils plus surfactant or mould cream emulsion.

Temporary formwork: ensure that formwork:

a. is accurately placed in correct position, true to line and level, dimensionally correct and grout tight;
b. faces in contact with concrete are clean and either well wetted without an accumulation of surplus water at bottom, or treated with a release agent.

Retention: retain formwork in position for not less than 7 days.

Striking: strike formwork without damaging concrete.

Method of measurement

Generally:
Measure the concrete surfaces of finished construction which require temporary support during casting.

FORMWORK—*continued*

Method of measurement—***continued***

Face of wall:
Make no deduction for voids not exceeding 5.00 m².

Rates for the following include

Formwork:
For adaptation to accommodate projecting pipes, reinforcing bars or the like.

For all cutting, splayed edges or the like.

Mortice:
For any shape.

For dishings, pockets, sinkings or the like.

Item	*Square Metre*	£
	Face of wall	
R63	vertical ...	23.00
R64	battered ...	27.60
	Edge of bed, path or paving, foundation, step or upstand	
R65	exceeding 1000 mm high ...	17.53
	Metre	
R66	not exceeding 250 mm high ...	5.29
R67	250 to 500 mm high ...	9.43
R68	500 to 1000 mm high ...	14.38
R69	Extra over formwork for recess, rebate or the like—*per 25 mm of girth* ...	0.70
	Curved formwork of any shape: price at the foregoing Rates multiplied by the following factors:	
R70	not exceeding 2 m radius ...	multiply by 1.75
R71	2 to 3 m radius ...	multiply by 1.50
R72	3 to 5 m radius ...	multiply by 1.25
R73	5 to 15 m radius ...	multiply by 1.05
R74	exceeding 15 m radius ...	no adjustment
R75	Formwork left in, multiply the foregoing Rates by 1.50.	

Item		1	2	3
		Depth		
		not exceeding 250 mm	250 to 500 mm	500 to 1000 mm
	Each	£	£	£
	Mortice			
R76	not exceeding 500 mm girth ...	4.72	5.84	10.35
R77	500 to 1000 mm girth ...	7.91	9.27	18.51
R78	ADD *for each additional 1000 mm of girth* ...	6.76	9.41	12.69

REINFORCEMENT

Specification

Supply: obtain all steel bar and fabric reinforcement from firms belonging to the UK Certification Authority for Reinforcing Steels (CARES) Scheme for firms of approved capability.

Tying wire: soft iron, 1.6 mm diameter.

Cover spacers: concrete (10 mm aggregate), cement and sand mortar (1:2) or proprietary plastic of approved type.

Inspect and reject bends and hooks showing signs of cracking or brittleness.

Accuracy: check information on bar bending schedules for compatability with drawings, report any discrepancies to the SO and obtain his instructions.

Cutting and Bending: comply with BS 4466.

Cold bending: bend bars on approved machines.

Hot bending: hot bend only with approval.

Re-bending: do not re-bend, bend after fixing or straighten any bars without approval.

Hooks: do not provide hooks unless ordered.

Positioning of reinforcement: secure reinforcement and maintain in proper positions with the correct cover as ordered by means of approved temporary or permanent chairs, spacers etc and ample use of tying wire. Bend back all ends of tying wire well clear of the formwork.

Placed concrete: do not insert any bars into placed concrete.

Method of measurement

Fabric reinforcement:
Measure net with no allowance made for laps.

Make no deduction for voids not exceeding 1.00 m².

Rates for the following include

Generally:
For spacers and tying wire.

Bar reinforement:
For cutting bars to lengths and forming hooked ends and bends where required.

For horizontal, sloping or vertical bars of any length.

Fabric reinforcement:
For all cutting.

Item	*Kilogramme*	£
	Hot Rolled steel bars to BS 4449: Mild Steel (Grade 250) round bars or High Yield Steel (Grade 460) deformed bars	
	other than links: straight, curved or bent	
R79	6 mm diameter	1.21
R80	8 mm diameter	1.09
R81	10 mm diameter	1.04
R82	12 mm diameter	0.92
R83	16 mm diameter	0.86
R84	20 and 25 mm diameter	0.81
	in links or the like: bent	
R85	6 mm diameter	1.27
R86	8 mm diameter	1.15
R87	10 mm diameter	1.09

REINFORCEMENT—*continued*

Item	*Square Metre*	1	2	3	4
		Nominal mass per m²			
		2.61 kg	3.41 kg	4.34 kg	6.72 kg
		£	£	£	£
R88	Steel fabric to BS 4483: long mesh fabric: 100 × 400 mm mesh: minimum 450 mm transverse laps (no longitudinal lap)	3.22	4.20	5.06	7.36
	strip: in one width				
R89	not exceeding 300 mm wide	4.03	5.29	6.38	9.26
R90	300 to 450 mm wide	3.73	4.95	5.92	8.63
R91	Bending	1.15	1.31	1.52	1.90

MOVEMENT JOINTS

Specification

Movement joint filler: knot free softwood or waterproof, compressible, non-extruding, pre-moulded filler with high recovery factor after compression at temperatures below 50°C.

Joint sealant: to BS 2499 type A2.

Preforming movement joints: prior to concreting, set rigidly in position and support to prevent displacement of joint filler, sealing groove fillet and;

a. maintain support until adjacent concrete has set before placing concrete for next slab;
b. keep sealing groove fillet in position until concrete on both sides of joint is fully cured;
c. remove fillet immediately prior to sealing joint.

Rounding on upper edges at joints: round upper edges of slabs at joints to 10 mm radius using bullnose arris trowel. Do not overwork concrete.

Placing softwood filler: immerse softwood filler in water for 48 hours, before placing in joint and keep damp prior to concreting.

Sealing grooves: remove sealing groove fillet, clean out groove and fill with sealing compound.

Item	*Metre*	£
	Movement joint: 25 mm thick filler: groove: formwork	
R92	not exceeding 150 mm deep	2.54
R93	150 to 300 mm deep	3.79
R94	300 to 450 mm deep	6.28
R95	Sealant: 25 × 25 mm	3.15

WORKED FINISHES/CUTTING

Rates for the following include

Worked finishes:
For producing by hand or mechanical means.

Making good:
For making good to match adjacent surfaces.

Cutting:
For cutting set or existing concrete.

Mortice:
For any shape.

For dishings, pockets, sinkings or the like.

Mortars:
For any mix.

WORKED FINISHES/CUTTING—*continued*

Item	*Square Metre*	£
R96	Tamped ribbed finish ...	0.63
R97	Rolled pattern finish ...	1.42
R98	Power floated finish to smooth, even surface ...	1.57
R99	Even textured finish achieved with scraping straight edge and medium coarse fibre broom ...	2.43
	ADD to the foregoing Rates where	
R100	sloping ...	0.63
R101	to falls or crossfalls ...	0.40

Item	*Metre*	1 Straight £	2 Curved £	3 ADD for making good £	4 ADD where in reinforced concrete £
R102	Cutting chase: not exceeding 100 mm girth ...	4.08	5.33	2.20	3.14
R103	ADD *for each additional 50 mm of girth* ...	2.04	2.67	0.94	1.57
R104	Cutting rebate: not exceeding 100 mm girth ...	3.45	4.71	1.96	3.14
R105	ADD *for each additional 50 mm of girth* ...	1.72	2.34	0.78	1.57
R106	Cutting chamfer: not exceeding 100 mm girth ...	2.82	4.08	2.13	3.14
R107	ADD *for each additional 50 mm of girth* ...	1.41	2.04	0.78	1.57

Item	*Each*	1 Not exceeding 100 mm deep £	2 100 to 200 mm deep £	3 200 to 300 mm deep £	4 ADD for making good £	5 ADD where in reinforced concrete £	6 ADD for grouting with mortar £	7 ADD for caulking with lead £
	Cutting mortice							
R108	not exceeding 2500 mm² ...	3.56	10.14	15.47	0.55	1.50	1.40	3.48
R109	2500 to 5000 mm² ...	3.93	11.45	16.79	0.88	1.60	1.40	3.61
R110	5000 to 7500 mm² ...	4.25	12.40	18.34	1.03	2.35	2.11	5.10
R111	7500 to 10000 mm² ...	4.62	13.40	19.66	1.36	3.14	2.11	5.35
R112	Cutting hole: not exceeding 2500 mm² ...	6.26	9.40	15.67	0.58	3.14	1.26	3.14
R113	ADD *for each additional 2500 mm²* ...	0.94	1.57	2.19	0.48	1.41	1.00	2.29

REPAIRS TO CONCRETE

Specification

Re-sealing movement joint groove:

a. Remove hardened joint material;
b. Remove all dust and debris by scraping or brushing;
c. Prime sides and bottoms of all joints with an approved solution as recommended by the manufacturer of the joint sealant;
d. Re-fill groove with joint sealant to BS 2499 type A2.

Repairing crack:

a. Remove all dust and debris by scraping or brushing;
b. Fill crack with latex rubber bitumen emulsion;
c. Dust surface with cement or fine sand.

Item	*Metre*	£
R114	Re-sealing movement joint groove: not exceeding 30 × 30 mm … … … … …	6.13
R115	Repairing crack: not exceeding 10 mm wide … … … … … … … …	3.14

FLEXIBLE SHEET MEMBRANES

Specification

Waterproof building paper:

a. to BS 1521;
b. loose lay in a single layer with minimum 150 mm laps.

Polythene sheet:

a. translucent or black opaque;
b. loose lay in a single layer with minimum 150 mm laps.

Definition

Horizontal:

Includes slopes not exceeding 10° from horizontal.

Method of measurement

Generally:

Measure area in contact with the base. Make no deduction for voids not exceeding 1.00 m².

Rates for the following include

Generally:

For all cutting, holing, notching and bending.

For extra material for laps.

		1	2
		Waterproof building paper: grade	
		AIF	BIF
	Square Metre	£	£
R116	Sheeting: horizontal: on ground, filling, sub-base or the like … … … …	0.81	0.70

		1	2	3	4	5
		Polythene sheet: gauge				
		250	500	1000	1200	2000
		£	£	£	£	£
R117	Sheeting: horizontal: on ground, filling, sub-base or the like … … … … … …	0.39	0.48	0.69	0.94	1.26

BRICKWORK

GENERALLY

Specification

Constituent materials for mortar:

a. Cement: to BS 12, BS 146 or BS 4027 and manufactured by a BSI Registered Firm.
b. Masonry cement: to BS 5224.
c. Sand: to BS 1200 Table 1.
d. Hydrated lime powder and lime putty: to BS 890.
e. Ready mixed lime/sand mix: to BS 4721 Section 2.
f. Plasticizer: to BS 4887 Part 1 and manufactured by a BSI Kitemark Licensee.
g. Pigments for coloured mortar: to BS 1014.
h. Water: clean and uncontaminated. Obtain approval for other than mains supply.

Mix Proportions: mix constituent materials in proportion by volume as the following Table:

Mortar Type

Type No.	BS Mortar Designation	A Cement: sand	B Cement: ready mixed lime/sand (proportions of lime and sand as given in brackets)		C Cement: sand with plasticizer	D Masonry cement: sand
1	(i)	1:3	1:3	(1:12)	—	—
2	(ii)	—	1:4½	(1:9)	1:3–4	—
3	(iii)	—	1:6	(1:6)	1:5–6	1:4–5
4	(iv)	—	1:9	(1:4½)	1:7–8	1:5½–6½
5	(v)	—	1:12	(1:4)	1:8	1:6½–7

Coloured Portland cement mortars: added pigments must not exceed 10% of the weight of the cement used, except for carbon black which must not exceed 3% by weight of cement.

Ready mixed mortar: to BS 4721 Part 3, mortar designation as specified for the Type No. scheduled in Table. Do not use for structural masonry without approval.

Site mixed mortar: mix in the proportions by volume as specified for the Type No. scheduled in Table.

Setting time: use mortars containing cement within two hours of mixing unless retardants have been added. Discard unused mortar.

Cold weather: do not mix mortar unless precautions are taken to ensure that it has a minimum temperature of 4°C when laid.

Finishing of mortar joints not visible: strike off with trowel as work proceeds joints not visible in finished work.

Definitions

Composite work: Walls etc built of more than one type of brick in the thickness of the wall.

Isolated pier: Isolated walls whose length on plan is not exceeding four times their thickness, except where caused by openings.

Projection: Attached piers (whose length on plan is not exceeding four times the thickness of projection), plinths, oversailing courses or the like.

Note

Work generally:
Vertical unless otherwise stated.

Method of measurement

Generally:
Measure brickwork on the centre line of the material unless otherwise stated. Make no deductions for voids not exceeding 0.10 m².

Building against other work and bonding to other work:
Measure where the other work is existing or consists of a differing material.

Extra over for facework:
Measure on the exposed face.

Rates for the following include

Generally:
For English or Flemish bond, or stretcher bond in the case of half-brick walls, unless otherwise stated.

For rough cutting new work *except* rounded or chamfered angles.

GENERALLY—*continued*

Rates for the following include—*continued*

Generally:—continued
For fair straight, raking or splay cutting new work.

For rough horizontal chases in new work.

Cement mortar:
For any of the mortars in Type 1 of the Mortar Type Table.

Cement-lime mortar:
For any of the mortars in Types 2, 3, 4 or 5 of the Mortar Type Table.

Any mortar:
For any mortar in the Mortar Type Table including mortar incorporating sulphate-resisting cement.

Curved work:
For extra material.

Building against other work:
For bedding in mortar.

Bonding to other work:
For extra material for bonding.

Bonding end of new wall to existing:
For any approved method of bonding to suit the particular circumstances.

For extra material for bonding and for cutting sockets.

Facework:
For selecting bricks with undamaged arrises and flat surfaces.

For finishing joints with flush, concave, weathered or recessed joint as the work proceeds unless otherwise stated.

Fair angle:
For vertical, raking or horizontal angles.

Threshold or coping:
For angles and ends.

Fair cutting brickwork:
For cutting not exceeding half-brick deep.

Making good existing facework:
For pointing to match existing.

COMMON BRICKWORK: LAYING ONLY: GENERALLY

Note

Number of bricks:
Calculate from the following Table:

Number of common bricks per square metre including waste

Thickness of wall	65 mm and 67 mm	73 mm
Half-brick stretcher bond...	65	59
Half-brick honeycomb bond...	39	35
One-brick	128	116
One-brick honeycomb bond...	78	70
One-and-a-half brick ...	191	173
ADD *for each additional half-brick thickness*	63	57
One-brick curved not exceeding 2 m radius	140	127
One-brick curved exceeding 2 m radius	134	122

For linear items calculate the actual number of bricks required and add 10 per cent for waste.

Rates for the following include

Generally:
For everything *except* the cost of bricks.

For laying new or old bricks of any of the following types:

a. Clay common bricks to BS 3921;
b. Calcium silicate common bricks to BS 187;
c. Approved common bricks as ordered, nominal size 219 × 105 × 67 or 73 mm.

COMMON BRICKWORK: LAYING ONLY: IN CEMENT-LIME MORTAR

Item	Square Metre	1 Brick thickness Half £	2 One £	3 One-and-a-half £	4 ADD *for each additional half-brick* £
R118	Wall	19.57	36.11	44.53	13.06
R119	Wall: honeycomb bond: one third area void	18.42	29.92	—	—
	ADD where				
R120	building against other work	3.15	3.15	3.15	—
	bonding to other work				
R121	forming pockets	2.30	2.30	2.30	—
R122	cutting pockets: in existing brickwork	5.52	5.52	5.52	—
	curved on plan				
R123	not exceeding 2 m radius	11.76	18.77	22.28	10.37
R124	exceeding 2 m radius	8.32	14.19	20.21	6.00
R125	curved bricks: not exceeding 2 m radius	14.64	23.40	—	—
R126	Isolated pier	—	44.68	62.00	16.26

Item	*Square Metre—per half-brick thickness*	£
	ADD where	
R127	in cement mortar	1.19
R128	sulphate-resisting cement used instead of ordinary cement	0.58

Item	*Metre-per half-brick width*	1 Brick projection Half £	2 One £	3 One-and-a-half £	4 ADD *for each additional half-brick* £
R129	Projection: horizontal or vertical	2.67	4.55	6.42	1.87
	ADD where bonding to other work				
R130	forming pockets	2.42	4.13	5.53	1.41
R131	cutting pockets: in existing brickwork	2.68	4.57	6.11	1.56

Item		£
	ADD where	
R132	in cement mortar	0.13
R133	sulphate-resisting cement used instead of ordinary cement	0.08

COMMON BRICKWORK: LAYING ONLY: IN CEMENT-LIME MORTAR—*continued*

Item	*Square Metre*	£
	Extra over for facework	
R134	exceeding half-brick wide	4.09
R135	exceeding half-brick wide: building overhand	6.21
R136	exceeding half-brick wide: curved on plan: not exceeding 2 m radius	4.49
R137	exceeding half-brick wide: curved on plan: exceeding 2 m radius	4.28
	Metre	
R138	not exceeding half-brick wide	1.26
R139	Fair chamfered or rounded external angle: any girth	3.34
	Each	
R140	end or mitre	0.74

COMMON BRICKWORK: LAYING ONLY: IN ANY MORTAR

Rates for the following include

Generally:
For facework to exposed faces.

		1	2	3
		Brick width		
		Half	One	One-and-a-half
	Metre	£	£	£
	Threshold or coping: raking or horizontal: square or rounded external angles: set level or weathering			
R141	brick on edge	–	10.83	14.28
	ADD where curved on plan			
R142	not exceeding 2 m radius	–	1.04	2.14
R143	exceeding 2 m radius	–	0.57	1.07
R144	brick on end	9.98	–	–
	ADD where curved on plan			
R145	not exceeding 2 m radius	0.83	–	–
R146	exceeding 2 m radius	0.41	–	–

COMMON BRICKWORK: SUNDRIES

Rates for the following include

Generally:
For everything *including* bricks.

For work in any mortar.

Making good existing facework:
For work to common brickwork or facing brickwork.

Item		1 New brickwork	2 Existing brickwork
	Square Metre	£	£
R147	Rough cutting	Incl	15.97
	Metre		
	Rough cutting rounded or chamfered angle		
R148	not exceeding 75 mm wide/girth	2.37	4.67
R149	75 to 150 mm wide/girth	3.15	5.72
	Fair cutting		
R150	to curve	4.64	9.29
R151	straight	Incl	3.63
R152	raking or splayed	Incl	6.96

Item		1 Thickness: Half-brick	2 One-brick	3 One-and-a-half brick	4 Not exceeding 300 mm hollow	5 ADD where making good existing facework—*per side*
		£	£	£	£	£
R153	Preparing top of existing wall for raising	1.19	2.40	3.58	2.36	—
R154	Bonding end of new wall to existing	5.58	10.89	15.97	11.75	1.88
R155	Making good with new brickwork: pockets in existing wall where old wall removed	9.21	15.02	18.51	17.72	—
R156	ADD for facework to new brickwork: to match existing	1.88	3.05	4.19	3.63	—

FACING BRICKWORK AND COMPOSITE WORK: LAYING ONLY: GENERALLY

Rates for the following include

Generally:
For everything *except* the cost of bricks.

For laying new or old bricks of any of the following types:
a. Clay facing bricks to BS 3921;
b. Calcium silicate facing bricks to BS 187;
c. Approved facing bricks as ordered, nominal size 219×105×67 or 73 mm.

For additional labour where facings of more than one type or colour are used in association.

For the even distribution of multi-coloured facings throughout the finished work.

Column A:
For jointing and pointing in cement-lime mortar.

Column B:
For jointing and pointing in white or coloured cement-lime mortar or with coal ash substituted for sand as ordered.

FACING BRICKWORK: LAYING ONLY

Note

Number of bricks:
Calculate from the following Table:

Number of facing bricks per square metre including waste

Thickness and bond of wall	65 mm or 67 mm	73 mm
Half-brick in stretcher bond...	62	56
Half-brick in English bond with snapped headers	62	56
One-brick in any bond	122	110

For linear items calculate the actual number of bricks required and add 5 per cent for waste.

Rates for the following include

Threshold or coping:
For facework to exposed faces.

Item	*Square Metre*	1 A £	2 B £
	Wall: half-brick thick		
	stretcher bond		
R157	facework one side	27.89	30.97
R158	facework both sides	30.80	34.21
	English bond		
R159	snapped headers: facework on side	32.65	36.26
R160	snapped headers: building against other work: facework one side	34.02	37.78
R161	ADD where in cement mortar	1.19	1.19
	Wall: one brick thick		
R162	garden wall bond: facework both sides	50.45	52.54
R163	English bond: facework both sides	50.63	52.83
R164	Flemish bond: facework both sides	50.82	53.10
R165	ADD where in cement mortar	2.39	2.39
	Metre		
	Extra for fair return		
R166	not exceeding half-brick wide	1.27	1.27
R167	half-brick to one-brick wide	1.90	1.90
R168	Fair chamfered or rounded external angle: any girth	3.34	3.34
	Each		
R169	end or mitre	0.74	0.74

FACING BRICKWORK: LAYING ONLY—*continued*

Item	*Metre—per half-brick width*	1 A £	2 B £
	Projection: facework to face and margins—*per half-brick projection from face of wall*		
R170	horizontal or vertical	4.01	4.43
	ADD where bonding to other work		
R171	forming pockets	3.64	3.64
R172	cutting pockets: in existing brickwork	4.03	4.03
	Metre		
	Threshold or coping: raking or horizontal: square or rounded external angles: set level or weathering		
	brick on edge		
R173	one-brick wide	12.28	12.70
	ADD where curved on plan		
R174	not exceeding 2 m radius	1.25	1.25
R175	exceeding 2 m radius	0.66	0.66
R176	one-and-a-half brick wide	17.43	17.61
	ADD where curved on plan		
R177	not exceeding 2 m radius	2.39	2.39
R178	exceeding 2 m radius	1.21	1.21
	brick on end		
R179	half-brick wide	11.52	11.87
	ADD where curved on plan		
R180	not exceeding 2 m radius	1.15	1.15
R181	exceeding 2 m radius	0.57	0.57

COMPOSITE WORK: LAYING ONLY: EXTRA OVER COMMON BRICKWORK IN CEMENT-LIME MORTAR FOR FACING BRICKWORK

Note

Number of bricks:
Calculate from the following Table:

Number of facing bricks per square metre including waste

Bond	Facing bricks and DEDUCT common bricks	
	65 mm and 67 mm	73 mm
English bond	92	82
English bond with snapped headers ...	62	56
Flemish bond	81	73
Flemish bond with snapped headers ...	62	56
ADD where curved on plan not exceeding 2 m radius	8	8
ADD where curved on plan exceeding 2 m radius	4	4

For linear items calculate the actual number of facing bricks required and add 5 per cent for waste. DEDUCT the same number of common bricks.

Method of measurement

Generally:
Measure on the exposed face.

Rates for the following include

Column B:
For the extra cost of providing Column B type mortar through the full thickness of the faced wall.

Item		1	2
		A	B
	Square Metre	£	£
	Facework: exceeding half-brick wide		
R182	English bond	10.07	11.82
R183	Flemish bond:	10.49	12.08
R184	English or Flemish bond with snapped headers	11.15	12.77
	ADD where		
R185	curved on plan: exceeding 2 m radius	1.02	1.29
R186	curved bricks: not exceeding 2 m radius	4.10	4.44
	Metre		
R187	Facework: not exceeding half-brick wide	1.64	2.19

FACING BRICKWORK AND COMPOSITE WORK: SUNDRIES

Rates for the following include

Generally:
For everything *including* bricks.

For work in any mortar.

Item	*Metre*	£
	Fair cutting	
R188	to curve	7.43
R189	squint angle	8.24

CHASES

		1	2
		Common brickwork or facing brickwork	
		New	Existing
	Metre	£	£
	Chase: not exceeding 150 mm deep		
R190	not exceeding 150 mm high: horizontal	Incl	9.88
R191	not exceeding 150 mm wide: vertical or raking	7.06	10.63
R192	150 to 225 mm high: horizontal	Incl	11.88
R193	150 to 225 mm wide: vertical or raking	8.18	12.26

MORTICES

		1	2	3
		Common brickwork or facing brickwork	ADD where making good facework	ADD where making good facework to facing brickwork
	Each	£	£	£
R194	Mortice for bolt or the like: not exceeding 25 mm diameter: not exceeding 100 mm deep	0.66	0.25	0.38
R195	ADD *for each additional 50 mm of depth*	0.33	0.13	0.22
R196	Mortice not exceeding 50 × 50 × 100 mm deep: grouting with mortar	1.34	0.49	0.74

DAMP PROOF COURSES

Specification

Bitumen damp proof course: to BS 6398 Type E.

Polyethylene damp proof courses: to BS 6515.

Pitch polymer damp proof course: from an approved manufacturer.

Lead damp proof course: to BS 743, Code 4, bitumen coated both sides.

Slate damp proof course: to BS 743.

Method of measurement

Generally:
Measure the area covered with no allowance for laps. Make no deduction for voids not exceeding 0.50 m².

Rates for the following include

Generally:
For bedding in cement mortar.

For pointing exposed edges.

Sheet damp proof courses:
For laying in single layer.

For laying with 150 mm laps in length and full lap at angles.

For dressing projecting edges up or down as ordered.

Slate damp proof course:
For laying in two courses breaking joint.

Curved work:
For all necessary cutting.

Sheet damp proof courses

Item	Square Metre	1	2	3	4	5
		Horizontal or stepped				ADD where vertical
		Bitumen	Poly-ethylene	Pitch polymer	Lead	
		£	£	£	£	£
	On surface					
R197	not exceeding 225 mm wide	11.22	7.23	14.30	37.52	3.21
R198	exceeding 225 mm wide	10.89	6.93	14.00	36.39	3.06

Slate damp proof courses

Item		1	2
		Horizontal or stepped	ADD where vertical
		£	£
	On surface		
R199	not exceeding 225 mm wide	44.00	5.65
R200	exceeding 225 mm wide	43.33	5.38

Sheet or slate damp proof courses

R201 Where curved on plan: price at the foregoing Rates multiplied by 1.20.

CRAMPS

Specification

Galvanised steel: to BS 4360 galvanised to BS 729.

Rates for the following include

Generally:
For any size or section shape.

Item	Each	£
R202	Coping cramp: bent: building in	0.56

NATURAL STONE RUBBLE WALLING

GENERALLY

Specification

Stone for random rubble walling: irregular shaped stones supplied with at least one bonder for each square metre of finished wall.

Preparation of stone: roughly shape stones to suit walling.

Mortar materials and mix proportions: as specified in the 'Brickwork' Sub-Section.

Mortar types: use the following mortar types detailed in the Mortar Type Table in the 'Brickwork' Sub-Section unless otherwise ordered:

Granite, quartzite or similar	Type 1
Dense sandstone and cast stone	Type 3
Limestone and porous sandstone	Type 4 or 5

Notes

Work generally:
Vertical unless otherwise stated.

Damp proof courses:
Pay for at the Rates in the 'Brickwork' Sub-Section.

Cramps:
Pay for at the Rates in the 'Brickwork' Sub-Section.

Method of measurement

Generally:
Measure mean dimensions. Make no deductions for voids not exceeding 0.10 m^2.

Bonding to other work:
Measure where the other work is existing or consists of a differing material.

Rates for the following include

Generally:
For everything *except* the cost of stone.

For any kind of stone of any profile.

For rough and fair square cutting.

For fair returns, ends, angles or the like on superficial items.

For ends, angles or the like on linear items.

Mortar:
For the use of coloured mortar, or substituting for sand, crushed stone or stone dust of the same type as the stone used.

Laying only stone previously set aside for re-use:
For cleaning off beds and joints and stacking prior to re-use.

Pointing:
For finishing joints by striking off flush as the work proceeds.

Bonding to other work:
For extra material for bonding.

Bonding end of new wall to existing:
For extra material for bonding and for cutting pockets.

STONEWORK: LAYING ONLY

Item	*Square Metre*	1 Laying only new stonework £	2 Laying only stonework previously set aside for re-use £
R203	Wall: random uncoursed: not exceeding 300 mm thick	39.81	43.03
R204	ADD *for each additional 50 mm of thickness*	3.17	3.38
	ADD where		
	bonding to other work		
R205	forming pockets	27.40	27.40
R206	cutting pockets: in existing stonework	28.24	28.24
R207	bringing to courses at average 750 mm vertical intervals—*per side*	3.29	3.29
R208	pointing—*per side*	3.42	3.42

STONEWORK: LAYING ONLY—*continued*

Item	Metre	1 Laying only new stonework £	2 Laying only stonework previously set aside for re-use £
R209	Coping: not exceeding 300 × 300 mm: horizontal: pointing exposed faces: levelling rubble walling	32.49	35.09
	ADD for		
R210	*each additional 50 mm of width*	4.60	4.97
R211	*each additional 50 mm of height*	4.05	4.36
R212	Bonding end of new wall to existing: not exceeding 300 mm thick	6.66	6.66
R213	ADD *for each additional 50 mm of thickness*	1.15	1.15
R214	Rough raking or circular cutting: not exceeding 300 mm thick	11.14	11.14
R215	ADD *for each additional 50 mm of thickness*	1.86	1.86
R216	Fair raking or circular cutting: not exceeding 300 mm thick	26.74	26.74
R217	ADD *for each additional 50 mm of thickness*	4.45	4.45

COATED MACADAM PAVINGS

GENERALLY

Method of measurement

Area:
Measure the area in contact with base. Make no deduction for voids not exceeding 0.50 m² or grounds.

Thickness:
Measure the compacted thickness exclusive of surface dressing.

Where laid over existing uneven paving, agree the average thickness with the SO before laying.

Rates for the following include

Generally:
For laying to falls, crossfalls, cambers or slopes not exceeding 15° from horizontal.

For forming or working into shallow channels and associated labours.

For laying on any new or existing base.

For preparing the base *except* forming key.

Work executed in small quantities

Where the total area of coated macadam surfacing executed in one location at the same time under one or more orders falls within the categories shown, multiply Rates R221 to R229 by the following factors:

R218	Not exceeding 10 m²	multiply by 3.00
R219	10 to 25 m²	multiply by 1.30

TACK COATS

Specification

Tack coat: to BS 434 Part 1.

Workmanship: comply with BS 434 Part 2 and BS 4987 Part 2, Clause 4.5.

Note

Use tack coat only where ordered.

Item	Square Metre	£
R220	Generally	0.61

COATED MACADAM

Specification

Coated macadam: manufacture, transport and lay in accordance with BS 4987 Parts 1 and 2.

Bitumen binder: penetration grade bitumen.

Coarse aggregate: crushed rock or slag.

Note

Clause references are to BS 4987 Part 1.

		1	2	3
		Thickness		
		20 mm	50 mm	ADD or DEDUCT *for each 5 mm variation in thickness*
	Square Metre	£	£	£
	Basecourse: bitumen macadam: 20 mm size			
R221	open graded: as Clause 6.1	—	5.31	0.40
R222	dense: as Clause 6.5	—	5.59	0.48
R223	Wearing course: bitumen macadam: 6 mm size: medium graded: as Clause 7.6	2.85	—	0.68

		£
R224	Blinding wearing course with coated grit as Clause 7.9	0.61

LABOURS ON COATED MACADAM

Rates for the following include

Generally:
For surfacing in any number of courses unless otherwise stated.

For surfacing of any description and any thickness.

Item	*Metre*	£
	Jointing to existing: cutting to line: coating with hot penetration grade bitumen	
R225	single course	0.63
R226	two course: trimming back wearing course to break joint: extra material	1.79
	Each	
R227	Working into recessed cover and around frame: any size	3.42
R228	Working around obstruction: not exceeding 0.30 m girth	1.03
R229	ADD *for each additional 0.30 m of girth*	0.45

REPAIRS TO COATED MACADAM

Specification

Repairing crack:
a. Remove all dust and debris by scraping and brushing.
b. Fill crack with latex rubber bitumen emulsion.
c. Dust surface with cement or fine sand.

Filling pot hole:
a. Cut out to full depth of original layer and trim back wearing course to break joint.
b. Remove all dust and debris by scraping and brushing.
c. Score surfaces and apply tack coat to bottom and sides.
d. Fill with new material to match existing.
e. Compact thoroughly so that patch conforms to existing surface and will not be further compacted by traffic.
f. Blind with coated grit where required to match existing surface.

Note

Filling pot holes exceeding 1.00 m²:
Measure and pay for at the Rates for new work.

Item	*Metre*	£
R230	Repairing crack: not exceeding 10 mm wide	3.14

Item		1	2	3	4
		Not exceeding 0.10 m²	0.10 to 0.25 m²	0.25 to 0.50 m²	0.50 to 1.00 m²
	Each	£	£	£	£
	Filling pot hole: any thickness				
R231	base course	2.32	4.24	7.90	12.16
R232	wearing course	2.11	3.87	7.23	11.21

PREFORMED PAVING

GENERALLY

Specification

Cement: to BS 12 or BS 146 and manufactured by a BSI Registered Firm.

Sand for mortar: to BS 1200 Table 1.

Mortar mix: cement and sand, 1:3 by volume.

Grout: ready mixed lime and sand, 1:3 by volume: to BS 4721, Section 2.

Sand for bedding: clean, sharp, hard (medium) grit sand containing not more than 3 per cent by weight passing a 63 micron BS sieve and not more than 10 per cent by weight retained on a 5 mm BS sieve.

Note

Beds:
Thicknesses stated are compacted thicknesses.

Method of measurement

Generally:
Measure area of exposed face.

Make no deduction for voids not exceeding 0.50 m^2.

Rates for the following include

Generally:
For cutting.

Fair joint to flush edge of existing paving:
For preparing edge of existing.

PRECAST CONCRETE AND STONE FLAGS

Specification

Concrete paving flags: hydraulically pressed concrete to BS 368, natural colour. Standard sizes as ordered.

Natural stone paving flags:

a. Stone: hard sound Yorkshire or Caithness or suitable local stone of equal quality. Prepare stone for laying on natural bed with surfaces out of winding.
b. Sizes: as ordered.
c. Finish:
   1. Yorkshire and similar stones: sawn with sawn edges.
   2. Caithness and similar stones: self-faced with all irregularities dressed off: edges carefully squared.

Mortar bed: minimum 25 mm thick.

Sand bed: minimum 40 mm thick.

Lay flags to an even surface, well pressed into bed in parallel courses to break joints by minimum of 150 mm.

Joints and jointing:

a. Joints to be even and approximately 10 mm wide.
b. Work grout well into joints.
c. Clean off surplus grout from surface of slabs.

Course and match flags with existing pavings.

		1	2	3	4	5	6	7	8
		Precast concrete				Stone			
		Supplying and laying		Laying only		Supplying and laying		Laying only	
		Thickness							
		50 mm	63 mm	50 mm	63 mm	50 mm	75 mm	50 mm	75 mm
Item	*Square Metre*	£	£	£	£	£	£	£	£
	Paving: regular rectangular sizes: level and to falls only: grouting joints								
R233	bedding on sand ...	14.27	16.16	6.34	8.09	91.49	115.52	8.16	11.13
R234	bedding on mortar ...	15.66	17.62	7.68	9.50	92.89	117.04	10.16	12.57

PRECAST CONCRETE AND STONE FLAGS—*continued*

		1	2	3	4	5	6	7	8
		Precast concrete				Stone			
		Supplying and laying		Laying only		Supplying and laying		Laying only	
		Thickness							
		50 mm	63 mm	50 mm	63 mm	50 mm	75 mm	50 mm	75 mm
Item	*Square Metre*	£	£	£	£	£	£	£	£
	Paving: random rectangular sizes: level and to falls only: grouting joints								
R235	bedding on sand ...	—	—	—	—	88.72	112.66	11.66	12.49
R236	bedding on mortar ...	—	—	—	—	90.04	114.16	13.66	13.95
R237	ADD where to falls and crossfalls and to slopes not exceeding 15° from horizontal	4.66	5.65	4.67	5.67	5.72	7.51	5.72	7.51
	ADD where in repairs								
R238	not exceeding 1 m^2 ...	6.15	7.55	6.15	7.55	7.55	9.97	7.55	9.97
R239	1 to 5 m^2	3.08	3.78	3.08	3.78	3.78	4.99	3.78	4.99
	Metre								
	Jointing to existing								
R240	regular size flags ...	6.16	7.53	2.52	2.98	6.85	8.90	2.64	3.44
R241	random size flags ...	—	—	—	—	8.58	10.72	2.86	3.56

		1	2	3
		Precast concrete or stone		
		Thickness		
		50 mm	63 mm	75 mm
	Each	£	£	£
R242	Cutting and fitting around obstruction: not exceeding 0.30 m girth	2.64	3.01	3.25
R243	ADD *for each additional 0.30 m of girth*	2.33	2.70	2.87

PEDESTRIAN DETERRENT PAVING

Specification

Paviors: precast concrete:

a. Pyramid pattern with smooth grey finish: size 600 × 600 × 75 mm thick; or
b. patterned to give appearance of natural quarried granite setts: colour black: size 600 × 600 × 65 mm thick.

Mortar bed: minimum 25 mm thick.

Sand bed: minimum 40 mm thick.

Joints and jointing:

a. Joints to be even and 3 to 4 mm wide.
b. Work grout well into joints.
c. Clean off surplus grout from surface of paviors.

Item		1	2	3	4
		Pyramid pattern		Granite sett pattern	
		Supplying and laying	Laying only	Supplying and laying	Laying only
	Square Metre	£	£	£	£
	Paving: level and to falls only: grouting joints				
R244	bedding on sand	37.05	11.68	35.87	8.11
R245	bedding on mortar	38.57	12.57	37.74	9.50
R246	ADD where to falls and crossfalls and to slopes not exceeding 15° from horizontal	7.51	7.51	5.65	5.65
	ADD where in repairs				
R247	not exceeding 1 m²	7.94	7.94	7.55	7.55
R248	1 to 5 m²	3.97	3.97	3.78	3.78
	Metre				
R249	Jointing to existing	8.90	3.44	7.53	2.98

Item		1	2
		Pyramid pattern	Granite sett pattern
	Each	£	£
R250	Cutting and fitting around obstruction: not exceeding 0.30 m girth	3.25	3.00
R251	ADD *for each additional 0.30 m of girth*	2.87	2.70

TACTILE PAVING

Specification

Tactile paving (paving for the blind):
Precast concrete: colour red: top finished with 25 mm diameter domes, 6 mm high.

Mortar bed: minimum 25 mm thick.

Sand bed: minimum 40 mm thick.

Lay slabs to an even surface and to a set pattern as ordered, well pressed into bed in parallel courses.

Joints and jointing:
a. Joints to be even and close fitting.
b. Work grout well into joints.
c. Clean off surplus grout from surface of slabs.

Course and match slabs with existing pavings.

Item		1	2	3	4
		Slab size			
		400 × 400 mm		450 × 450 mm	
		Supplying and laying	Laying only	Supplying and laying	Laying only
	Square Metre	£	£	£	£
	Paving: 50 mm thick: level and to falls only: grouting joints				
R252	bedding on sand	21.71	6.67	19.30	6.35
R253	bedding on mortar	23.10	8.06	20.68	7.68
R254	ADD where to falls and crossfalls and to slopes not exceeding 15° from horizontal	5.19	5.19	4.93	4.93
	ADD where in repairs				
R255	not exceeding 1 m²	6.85	6.85	6.51	6.51
R256	1 to 5 m²	3.43	3.43	3.26	3.26
	Metre				
R257	Jointing to existing	6.15	2.52	5.46	2.40

Item	*Each*	£
R258	Cutting and fitting around obstruction: not exceeding 0.30 m girth	2.64
R259	ADD *for each additional 0.30 m of girth*	2.33

GRANITE SETTS

Specification

Setts: to BS 435:
a. Size: 125 mm deep: any width: any length.
b. Finish: square hammer dressed.

Lay setts on 50 mm bed of mortar with 12 mm joints and grout.

Rates for the following include

Granite sett paving in fan-shaped pattern in concentric arcs:
For all half setts to achieve pattern.

Item		1 Supplying and laying	2 Laying only
	Square Metre	£	£
	Paving: level and to falls only		
R260	in parallel courses with joints alternately broken and touching	57.54	19.98
R261	in fan-shaped pattern in concentric arcs	68.14	33.26
R262	ADD where to falls and crossfalls and to slopes not exceeding 15° from horizontal	2.90	2.90
	ADD where in repairs		
R263	not exceeding 1 m^2	17.18	17.18
R264	1 to 5 m^2	8.59	8.59
	Metre		
R265	Jointing to existing	2.07	2.07

Item	*Each*	£
R266	Cutting and fitting around obstruction: not exceeding 0.30 m girth	3.50
R267	ADD *for each additional 0.30 m of girth*	1.90

COBBLESTONES

Specification

Cobbles: selected hard water-smoothed stones free from deleterious substances and in the size range 50 to 75 mm.

Hoggin base: compacted and levelled fine hoggin: minimum 75 mm thick.

Lean concrete base:
a. Grade 10 N/mm²: 20 to 40 mm aggregate.
b. Cement content: not less than 4 per cent by weight of dry aggregate.
c. Thickness: minimum 75 mm.

Laying cobbles: lay to pattern ordered. Hammer cobbles in by hand to a depth of 60 per cent of their length so that tops are level and to a uniform finish.

Joints and jointing: sprinkle a dry mix of mortar over cobbles to form a 5 mm skin over exposed base. Brush with soft brush to expose tops of cobbles to required amount and sprinkle water to set.

Item		1 Suppling and laying	2 Laying only
	Square Metre	£	£
	Paving: level and to falls only		
R268	hoggin base	45.73	32.66
R269	lean concrete base	46.76	37.11
R270	ADD where to falls and crossfalls and to slopes not exceeding 15° from horizontal	2.90	2.90
	ADD where in repairs		
R271	not exceeding 1 m²	28.09	28.09
R272	1 to 5 m²	14.05	14.05
	Metre		
R273	Jointing to existing	3.37	3.37

Item	*Each*	£
R274	Cutting and fitting around obstruction: not exceeding 0.30 m girth	3.75
R275	ADD *for each additional 0.30 m of girth*	2.04

PRECAST CONCRETE BLOCK PAVIORS

Specification

Block paviors and mitre blocks: manufactured in accordance with BS 6717 Part 1: chamfered on top edges: manufacturer's standard colours;

a. paviors: size 200 × 100 mm;

b. mitre blocks: triangular: size 200 × 191 mm overall.

Bed paviors and mitre blocks on sand minimum 50 mm thick.

Pattern: lay to a regular stretcher bond pattern aligned with main margins or to a regular herringbone pattern with mitre block margins.

Joints: close fitting with sand well brushed in.

Rates for the following include

Generally:
For margins.

Item		1	2	3	4	5	6
		Supplying and laying			Laying only		
		Thickness					
		65 mm	80 mm	100 mm	65 mm	80 mm	100 mm
	Square Metre	£	£	£	£	£	£
	Paving: level and to falls only						
R276	stretcher bond pattern	26.57	29.19	33.46	18.85	20.24	22.34
R277	herringbone pattern	29.44	32.28	36.87	21.72	23.33	25.75
R278	ADD where to falls and crossfalls and to slopes not exceeding 15° from horizontal	2.90	2.90	2.90	2.90	2.90	2.90
	ADD where in repairs						
R279	not exceeding 1 m²	16.09	17.55	19.36	16.09	17.55	19.36
R280	1 to 5 m²	8.05	8.78	9.68	8.05	8.78	9.68
	Metre						
R281	Jointing to existing	2.11	2.32	2.67	1.50	1.61	1.78

Item		1	2	3
		Thickness		
		65 mm	80 mm	100 mm
	Each	£	£	£
R282	Cutting and fitting around obstruction: not exceeding 0.30 m girth	2.74	2.94	3.25
R283	ADD *for each additional 0.30 m of girth*	1.48	1.59	1.76

LAYING ONLY BRICK PAVING

Specification

Bed bricks on mortar minimum 20 mm thick.

Pattern: lay to a regular stretcher bond pattern aligned with main margins or to a regular herringbone pattern, neatly splay cut at margins.

Joints: make joints approximately 10 mm wide and fill with bedding mortar to a flush surface.

Notes

Calculate the number of bricks from the following Table:

Number of brick per square metre including waste

Laid	Thickness 35 or 50 mm	65 or 67 mm	73 mm
Flat	40	40	40
On edge	—	62	56

Rates for the following include

Generally:
For everything *except* the cost of bricks.

For laying new or old bricks of any of the following types:

a. Clay facing bricks or engineering bricks Class A or B to BS 3921; standard format work size 215 × 102.5 × 65 mm.
b. Calcium silicate facing bricks to BS 187; work size 215 × 102.5 × 65 mm.
c. Approved facing or engineering bricks as ordered; nominal size 219 × 105 × 67 or 73 mm.
d. Clay pavior bricks to BS 3921; standard format work size 215 × 105 × 35 or 50 mm.

For plain border, one brick wide.

Facing bricks:
For additional labour where facings of more than one type or colour are used in association.

For the even distribution of multi-coloured facings throughout the finished work.

Item		1 Clay pavior bricks	2 Facing or engineering bricks
	Square Metre	£	£
	Paving: level and to falls only		
	laid flat		
R284	stretcher bond pattern	18.85	19.56
R285	herringbone pattern	21.72	22.43
	laid on edge		
R286	stretcher bond pattern	22.80	24.25
R287	herringbone pattern	26.69	28.13
R288	ADD where to falls and crossfalls and to slopes not exceeding 15° from horizontal	2.90	2.90
	ADD where in repairs		
R289	not exceeding 1 m²	15.53	16.09
R290	1 to 5 m²	7.76	8.04
	Metre		
R291	Jointing to existing	1.50	1.79
	Each		
R292	Cutting and fitting around obstruction: not exceeding 0.30 m girth	2.74	3.42
R293	ADD *for each additional 0.30 m of girth*	1.47	1.84

WORK TO OLD BRICK PAVING

Item	*Square Metre*	£
	Raking out decayed joints not less than 10 mm deep: repointing with a neat flush joint in mortar	
R294	bricks laid flat ...	5.58
R295	bricks laid on edge ...	6.41
	Metre	
R296	Raking out detached joint: 10 mm deep: repointing with a neat flush joint in mortar ...	0.67

GRAVEL, CLINKER AND HOGGIN PAVINGS

Specification

Harding binding gravel: 20 mm maximum size, containing a preponderance of angular material free from an excess of clay and sufficient grit to enable adequate compaction by rolling.

Clinker: approved well-graded clinker, 40 mm maximum size, free from deleterious substances and excess dust.

Fine hoggin: a combination of naturally occurring gravel, sand and clay with a minimum of 85 per cent by weight passing a 10 mm BS sieve.

Spreading and compacting paving: evenly spread and compact by 1.5 tonne minimum weight roller to required compacted thickness and levels.

Method of measurement

Generally:
Measure area in contact with base.

Make no deduction for voids not exceeding 0.50 m².

Measure the compacted thickness.

Rates for the following include

Generally:
For working over and around obstructions.

		1	2	3
		Gravel	Clinker	Hoggin
	Square Metre	£	£	£
	Paving: 50 mm thick			
R297	level and to falls only ...	2.28	2.19	2.15
R298	to falls and crossfalls and to slopes not exceeding 15° from horizontal ...	2.58	2.49	2.37
R299	ADD *for each additional 25 mm of thickness* ...	0.22	0.19	0.19
	ADD where in repairs			
R300	not exceeding 1m² ...	0.12	0.12	0.12
R301	1 to 5 m² ...	0.06	0.06	0.06

SPECIAL PAVINGS

GRASS BLOCK PAVING

Specification

Precast concrete perforated blocks: 406 × 406 × 103 mm deep blocks suitable for traffic up to 3 tonnes.

Plastic perforated formers: 600 × 600 × 100 mm deep formers for in situ concrete suitable for traffic up to 10 tonnes.

Sand blinding: 10 to 20 mm thick.

Concrete: 30 N/mm^2: 10 mm maximum size aggregate.

Reinforcement: mesh to BS 4483 Ref 193 weighing 3.02 kg/m^2.

Expansion joints: 25 × 100 mm wrought softwood at 10 m centres.

Soil filling: selected topsoil brushed into perforations.

Grass seed: selected grass seed as ordered.

Laying: lay blocks fully interconnected and to an even surface.

Note

Supplying grass seed:
Pay for separately.

Rates for the following include

Generally:
For laying blocks or formers on sand bed.

For burning out tops of plastic formers after 48 hours.

For brushing topsoil into perforations.

For sowing and raking grass seed.

Item	*Square Metre*	£
R302	Precast concrete perforated blocks: level and to falls only	24.60
R303	100 mm thick in situ concrete laid on and worked around plastic formers: reinforcement: brushing surface of concrete: level and to falls only	23.20

COCKLE-SHELL PAVING

Specification

Cockle-shells:
Approximately 25 mm diameter. Obtain from an approved supplier.

Spread evenly and lightly rake over to give an even finished surface.

Method of measurement

Generally:
Measure area in contact with base.

Make no deduction for voids not exceeding 0.50 m^2.

Measure the thickness as laid.

Rates for the following include

Generally:
For working over and around obstructions.

Item	*Square Metre*	£
R304	Paving: 50 mm thick: level and to falls only	2.20
R305	ADD *for each additional 25 mm of thickness*	0.85
R306	ADD where to falls and crossfalls not exceeding 15° from horizontal	0.05
	ADD where in repairs	
R307	not exceeding 1 m^2	0.10
R308	1 to 5 m^2	0.05

BARK/WOOD PAVING COVERINGS

Specification

Bark/wood products:
Obtain from an approved supplier.

Lay in accordance with supplier's recommendations.

Bark chips to paths:
Clean conifer or hardwood chips: particle size 5 to 30 mm.

Wood-fibre to paths:
Clean pulverised softwood with a low bark content: particle size not exceeding 30 mm.

Bark chips to play areas:
Clean conifer chips with minimal wood content: particle size 10 to 50 mm.

Planings of wood and bark to play areas:
10 to 110 mm long, 10 to 45 mm wide and 1 mm thick. Use under and around fixed structures.

Method of measurement

Generally:
Measure area in contact with base.

Make no deduction for voids not exceeding 0.50 m².

Measure the thickness as laid.

Rates for the following include

Generally:
For working over and around obstructions.

		1	2	3	4	5	6	7	8
		Conifer				Hardwood			
		Thickness							
		100 mm	150 mm	200 mm	250 mm	100 mm	150 mm	200 mm	250 mm
Item	*Square Metre*	£	£	£	£	£	£	£	£
R309	Bark chips to path: level and to falls only	2.95	4.22	5.45	6.70	3.15	4.52	5.85	7.21
R310	ADD where to falls and crossfalls and to slopes not exceeding 15° from horizontal	0.08	0.10	0.13	0.16	0.08	0.10	0.13	0.16
	ADD where in repairs								
R311	not exceeding 1 m²	0.10	0.13	0.17	0.21	0.10	0.13	0.17	0.21
R312	1 to 5 m²	0.05	0.07	0.08	0.11	0.05	0.07	0.08	0.11

		1	2	3	4	5
		Thickness				
		50 mm	100 mm	150 mm	200 mm	250 mm
		£	£	£	£	£
R313	Wood-fibre to path: level and to falls only ...	1.78	3.05	4.37	5.65	6.96
R314	ADD where to falls and crossfalls and to slopes not exceeding 15° from horizontal ...	0.05	0.08	0.10	0.13	0.16
	ADD where in repairs					
R315	not exceeding 1 m²	0.07	0.10	0.13	0.17	0.21
R316	1 to 5 m²	0.04	0.05	0.07	0.08	0.11

BARK/WOOD PAVING COVERINGS—*continued*

Item	*Square Metre*	1	2	3	4	5	6
		Thickness					
		50 mm	100 mm	150 mm	200 mm	250 mm	300 mm
		£	£	£	£	£	£
R317	Bark chips to play area: level and to falls only	—	4.85	7.10	9.25	11.47	13.67
R318	ADD where to falls and crossfalls and to slopes not exceeding 15° from horizontal	—	0.08	0.10	0.13	0.16	0.20
	ADD where in repairs						
R319	not exceeding 1 m²	—	0.10	0.13	0.17	0.21	0.25
R320	1 to 5 m²	—	0.05	0.07	0.08	0.11	0.13
R321	Planings of wood and bark to play area: level and to falls only	1.60	2.75	3.90	5.05	6.20	7.35
R322	ADD where to falls and crossfalls and to slopes not exceeding 15° from horizontal	0.05	0.08	0.10	0.13	0.16	0.20
	ADD where in repairs						
R323	not exceeding 1 m²	0.07	0.10	0.13	0.17	0.21	0.25
R324	1 to 5 m²	0.04	0.05	0.07	0.08	0.11	0.13

TREE GRILLES: PRECAST CONCRETE

Specification

Perforated tree grille slabs: precast concrete: from an approved manufacturer.

Kerbs: to match paving; 'L' shaped; each 496 × 496 × 50 mm thick × 150 mm high overall, in pairs linked with galvanised staples, to form one complete square enclosure: smooth grey finish.

Sand bed:
Minimum 25 mm thick.

Lay grille slabs to an even surface well pressed into bed in parallel courses.

Joints and jointing:
a. close jointed and run sand into joint;
b. brush surplus sand from grilles.

Item	*Each*	£
	Tree grille slab	
R325	496 × 496 × 50 mm thick: smooth grey finish	7.67
R326	ADD where with exposed aggregate	8.94
R327	600 × 300 × 50 mm thick: smooth grey or white finish	7.53
R328	Kerb: pair to form square enclosure: 2000 mm girth overall	25.49

EDGINGS

GENERALLY

Specification

Cement: ordinary or rapid hardening Portland cement to BS 12.

Sand: to BS 1200 Table 1.

Mortar: cement-sand (1:3).

Notes

Excavation and filling:
Pay for at the appropriate Rates in the 'Excavation and Filling' Sub-Section.

Concrete bed, haunching and formwork:
Pay for separately under Item R339.

PRECAST CONCRETE

Specification

Precast concrete: to BS 340: any finish: natural colour.

Laying edges: bed on concrete base, haunch with concrete and:

a. with vertical joints close fitting, unpointed, not exceeding 3 mm in width;
b. to line and levels vertically and horizontally with a tolerance of 3 mm.

Item	*Metre*	1 50 × 150 mm £	2 50 × 205 mm £	3 50 × 255 mm £	4 Fixing only: not exceeding 50 × 255 mm £
R329	Edging: square, chamfered, rounded or bullnosed	3.85	4.27	4.58	2.47
R330	ADD for curved units: any radius	0.26	0.29	0.31	0.17

BRICKWORK: LAYING ONLY

Note

Number of bricks:
Calculate the actual number of bricks required and add 5 per cent for waste.

Rates for the following include

Generally:
For everything *except* the cost of the bricks.

For laying new or old bricks of any of the following types:

a. Clay common, engineering or facing bricks to BS 3921;
b. Approved common, engineering or facing bricks as ordered, nominal size 219 × 105 × 67 or 73 mm.

For facework to exposed faces.

For bedding bricks on mortar minimum 20 mm thick.

For jointing and pointing in mortar.

BRICKWORK: LAYING ONLY—*continued*

Item	*Metre*	1 Common brickwork £	2 Engineering brickwork £	3 Facing brickwork £
	Edging: single course			
R331	stretchers: half brick wide	6.66	8.17	7.56
	ADD where curved on plan			
R332	not exceeding 2 m radius	0.64	0.64	0.64
R333	exceeding 2 m radius	0.32	0.32	0.32
R334	brick on edge: one brick wide	10.83	13.27	12.29
	ADD where curved on plan			
R335	not exceeding 2 m radius	1.04	1.04	1.04
R336	exceeding 2 m radius	0.57	0.57	0.57

GRANITE SETTS

Specification

Setts: to BS 435, square hammer dressed finish.

Lay setts on a bed of mortar with 12 mm joints and grout in with mortar.

Item	*Metre*	1 100 × 100 × 100 mm long £	2 100 × 125 × 200 mm long £	3 Laying only: not exceeding 100 × 125 × 200 mm long £
	Sett string course			
R337	single row	9.19	10.29	4.59
R338	double row	16.92	19.27	7.75

IN SITU CONCRETE: FORMWORK

Specification

Concrete: 20 N/mm²: 20 mm aggregate.

Item	*Cubic Metre*	£
R339	Concrete foundation, bed or haunching: formwork	152.66

SAWN SOFTWOOD

Specification

Edging and pegs:
Sawn softwood, preservative treated with creosote.

Nail edging to driven pegs with galvanised nails.

Rates for the following include

Generally:
For extra pegs at angles and intersections.

Item	*Metre*	£
	Edging: 50 × 50 mm pegs with pointed ends at 1000 mm centres	
R340	38 × 100 mm: 300 mm long pegs	3.93
R341	38 × 150 mm: 300 mm long pegs	5.76
R342	50 × 200 mm: 450 mm long pegs	7.33
R343	50 × 300 mm: 450 mm long pegs	9.20

CLEFT SOFTWOOD

Specification

Edgings:
Softwood logs minimum 125 mm or 150 mm diameter as ordered cleft to half round profile, stripped of bark and pressure preservative treated.

Pegs: of matching profile with slightly chamfered top.

Nail edging to driven pegs with galvanised nails.

Rates for the following include

Generally:
For extra pegs at angles and intersections.

Item	*Metre*	£
	Edging: two logs on edge high: 600 mm long pegs with pointed ends at 1200 mm centres	
R344	250 mm high	6.64
R345	300 mm high	7.14

PAVING MARKINGS

GENERALLY

Method of measurement

Broken lines:
Measure net.

Letters, numerals, symbols, arrows or the like:
Measure the girth along the centre line.

Rates for the following include

Generally:
For setting out in the position directed.

For straight or curved work.

For work on new or old non-porous surfacing or paving of any description.

For tack coat where directed.

For any colour.

MARKING PAINT

Specification

Chlorinated rubber paint: obtain from an approved manufacturer.

Epoxy resin paint: two-pack type from an approved manufacturer. Apply strictly in accordance with manufacturer's recommendations.

Obliterate painted markings by over-painting with black chlorinated rubber paint.

Item		1	2	3	4	5
		Chlorinated rubber		Epoxy resin		Obliterating with black chlorinated rubber paint
		New	Previously painted	New	Previously painted	
	Square Metre	£	£	£	£	£
R346	Any marking: exceeding 300 mm wide ...	7.33	5.63	8.25	6.56	5.37
	Metre					
R347	Line: not exceeding 100 mm wide	0.99	0.71	1.10	0.81	0.63
R348	Broken line: not exceeding 100 mm wide ...	1.37	0.93	1.49	1.05	0.82
R349	Letter, numeral, symbol, arrow or the like: not exceeding 100 mm wide	2.09	1.37	2.21	1.47	1.14
R350	ADD to Items R347 to R349 *for each additional 25 mm of width*	0.21	0.18	0.24	0.21	0.12

THERMOPLASTIC MATERIAL

Specification

Thermoplastic road marking material: to BS 3262 and manufactured by a BSI Kitemark Licensee.

Application of thermoplastic road markings: apply in the following thicknesses:

a. Synthetic hydrocarbon resin bound materials:
   1. screed lines: 2 to 5 mm;
   2. sprayed lines other than yellow: 1.5 mm;
   3. sprayed yellow lines: 0.8 mm.

b. Gum or wood resin bound materials:
   1. screed lines: 3 to 5 mm;
   2. sprayed lines other than yellow: 2 mm;
   3. sprayed yellow lines: 2 to 3 mm.

THERMOPLASTIC MATERIAL—*continued*

Item		1	2	3	4
		New	Previously painted	Removing or obliterating existing markings	
				removing by approved method: making good surfaces	painting over with black chlorinated rubber paint
	Square Metre	£	£	£	£
R351	Any marking: exceeding 300 mm wide	11.63	10.88	4.00	5.37
	Metre				
R352	Line: not exceeding 100 mm wide	1.20	1.14	0.50	0.63
R353	Broken line: not exceeding 100 mm wide	1.53	1.43	0.60	0.83
R354	Letter, numeral, symbol, arrow or the like: not exceeding 100 mm wide	2.43	1.68	0.60	1.14
R355	ADD to Items R352 to R354 *for each additional 25 mm of width*	0.38	0.33	0.12	0.12

STONE FILLED FIREBREAKS

Specification

Broken or crushed stone chippings:
Obtain from an approved manufacturer.

Weedkiller: as ordered and applied strictly in accordance with the directions in the 'Fertilizers, Pesticides and Top Dressing' Section.

Notes

Supplying weedkiller:
Pay for separately.

Edgings:
Pay for at the appropriate Rates in the 'Edgings' Sub-Section.

Rates for the following include

Generally:
For forming against buildings, fences or the like.

For disposing surplus excavated material.

Item	*Metre*	£
	Excavating trench for firebreak 150 mm deep: trimming edges to a straight and even line: filling with stone chippings: raking surface level: applying weedkiller	
R356	500 mm wide	5.16
R357	1000 mm wide	9.55

WEED-FREE BASE FOR COILED BARBED OR RAZOR WIRE

Specification

Gravel:
Obtain from an approved manufacturer.

Weedkiller: as ordered and applied strictly in accordance with the directions in the 'Fertilizers, Pesticides and Top Dressing' Section.

Notes

Supplying weedkiller:
Pay for separately.

Edgings:
Pay for at the appropriate Rates in the 'Edgings' Sub-Section.

Rates for the following include

Generally:
For disposing surplus excavated material.

Item	*Metre*	£
	Excavating trench 225 mm deep: trimming edges to straight or curved line: filling with gravel: raking surface level: applying weedkiller	
R358	1750 mm wide	12.93
R359	2000 mm wide	14.78

MAINTENANCE OF PAVED AREAS

LEAF CLEARANCE

	100 Square Metres	£
	Clearing paved area of leaves and other extraneous debris: removing and depositing arisings: using	
R360	equipment mounted on or towed by tractor	0.12
R361	self propelled brush/vacuum machine	0.35
R362	pedestrian operated self-powered equipment	0.44
R363	hand implement	0.59
	ADD for	
R364	burning arisings	0.07
R365	disposing arisings	0.13

LITTER CLEARANCE

	100 Square Metres	£
R366	Picking up and collecting litter: disposing	0.29

GRAVEL OR COCKLE-SHELL PAVING

Rates for the following include

Generally:
For collecting weeds and debris, removing and depositing and leaving area tidy.

Item	*100 Square Metres*	£
R367	Raking over surface	3.15
R368	Hand weeding	18.80
R369	Hand hoeing: not exceeding 25 mm deep	12.55

REMOVAL OF SNOW AND ICE

Specification

Rock salt: from an approved supplier.

Store salt in containers which allow no percolation or seepage, at least 15 m away from cultivated, planted or grassed areas.

Spread evenly at the rate ordered and keep off adjacent cultivated, planted or grassed areas. Replace at Contractor's expense all plants, grass etc damaged by salt application.

Definitions

Precautionary treatment:
Treatment of surfaces prior to frost or snow-fall.

Clearance treatment:
Treatment of surfaces after snow-fall not exceeding 25 mm deep.

Note

Supplying rock salt:
Pay for separately.

Rates for the following include

Generally:
For transporting salt from site storage.

For spreading to paths, paved areas, ramps, steps or landings.

For spreading by means of a mechanical spreader or by hand implements.

For spreading at the coverage rates ordered.

Item	*100 Square Metres*	£
R370	Precautionary treatment—*per kilogramme per 100 m²*	0.42
R371	Clearance treatment—*per kilogramme per 100 m²*	0.47

S: Street Furniture

GENERALLY

Notes

Ground-fixed and floor mounted items:
Heights stated are the overall heights above ground.

Free-standing items:
Heights stated are the overall heights above ground (including plinths where applicable).

Rates for the following include

Generally:
For moving items from delivery point or existing location and re-siting as ordered within the site.

For assembling (where appropriate) and fixing in accordance with manufacturer's instructions.

Ground-fixed items:
For excavating holes for supports, bases, etc and disposing of arisings.

For breaking through existing hard surfacings.

For setting into ground at depth recommended by the manufacturer or as ordered.

For setting horizontally, vertically or raking as appropriate or as ordered.

For filling holes for supports, bases, etc with concrete (10 N/mm^2: 40 mm maximum size aggregate) to the full depth.

Floor- or wall-mounted items:
For fixing with bolts to any background.

For grouting holding down bolts with cement mortar.

Free-standing items:
For plinth units where applicable.

For placing in position as ordered.

BOLLARDS: FIXING ONLY

Item	Each	1 Maximum diameter 200 to 300 mm £	2 Maximum diameter 300 to 400 mm £
	Bollard: straight or tapered: ground-fixed		
	precast concrete: any finish: height		
S1	not exceeding 500 mm	12.65	16.85
S2	500 to 750 mm	13.15	17.45
S3	750 to 1000 mm	13.75	19.15

Item	Each	£
	mild steel hollow section: height not exceeding 1000 mm: not exceeding	
S4	150 × 150 mm	7.01
S5	200 mm diameter	8.60

PLANT CONTAINERS: FIXING ONLY

Notes

Supplying filling materials:
Pay for separately.

Planting:
Pay for at the appropriate Rates in the 'Trees, Shrubs and Other Plants' Section.

Rates for the following include

Filling containers:
For filling with drainage material, soil, compost or other approved material and preparing for planting.

Method of measurement

Planting area:
Measure as the surface area of the filling material.

Item	*Each*	1	2	3	4
		Planting area			
		not exceeding 0.50 m²	0.50 to 1.00 m²	1.00 to 1.50 m²	1.50 to 2.00 m²
		£	£	£	£
	Plant container: any shape: free-standing				
	precast concrete: height				
S6	not exceeding 500 mm	4.18	6.27	8.36	12.54
S7	500 to 750 mm	6.27	8.36	12.54	14.74
S8	ADD *for each additional 250 mm of height*	1.25	1.88	2.51	3.76
	glass reinforced cement: height				
S9	not exceeding 500 mm	3.13	5.22	7.31	9.40
S10	500 to 750 mm	5.22	7.31	9.40	11.49
S11	ADD *for each additional 250 mm of height*	0.94	1.56	2.19	2.82
	glass reinforced plastics: height				
S12	not exceeding 500 mm	2.09	3.14	4.18	6.27
S13	500 to 750 mm	3.14	4.18	6.27	7.37
S14	ADD *for each additional 250 mm of height*	0.63	0.94	2.51	1.88

Item	*Cubic Metre*	£
S15	Filling containers	8.20

LITTER BINS: FIXING ONLY

Definition

Capacity (precast concrete units):
Manufacturer's specified capacity.

Rates for the following include

Generally:
For inserting inner basket or liner (where applicable).

Item	*Each*	£
	Litter bin	
	precast concrete: any shape: free-standing: capacity	
S16	not exceeding 100 litres	3.15
S17	100 to 200 litres	4.18
S18	exceeding 200 litres	6.27
S19	hardwood: floor mounted: not exceeding 500 × 500 × 800 mm high	4.60

Item		1 Ground-fixed £	2 Floor-mounted £
	mild steel: pedestal type: not exceeding 500 mm diameter overall		
	two-piece: lockable top section: padlock: hand two keys to S.O.		
	medium duty: height		
S20	not exceeding 750 mm	7.20	5.10
S21	750 to 900 mm	8.90	6.30
S22	heavy duty: height not exceeding 750 mm	10.76	7.62
S23	one-piece: heavy duty: height not exceeding 750 mm	10.50	7.44

CYCLE STANDS: FIXING ONLY

Rates for the following include

Paving type cycle blocks:
For any additional filling under to bring flush with surrounding paving.

Free-standing type cycle blocks:
For bedding in cement and sand (1:3).

Item	*Each*	£
	Cycle block: precast concrete	
	paving type: 100 mm thick	
S24	600 × 300 mm	4.94
S25	500 × 500 mm	5.56
S26	free-standing type: 590 × 210 × 280 mm high	7.42

Item		1 Ground-fixed £	2 Floor-mounted £	3 Wall-mounted £
S27	Cycle parking stand: galvanised mild steel: 915 mm high: not exceeding 1500 mm long: two fixing points	11.75	—	—
	Front wheel support: galvanised mild steel			
S28	275 mm high: single sided for one bicycle	—	—	4.30
	515 mm high			
S29	single sided for one bicycle	7.20	5.10	—
S30	double sided for two bicycles	7.90	5.60	—
	Range of front wheel supports: 3000 mm long galvanised mild steel frame			
S31	330 mm high: single sided for five bicycles	—	—	18.30
	515 mm high			
S32	single sided for six bicycles	20.05	14.20	—
S33	double sided for twelve bicycles	22.59	16.00	—

BENCHES AND SEATS: FIXING ONLY

Item	*Each*	£
	Seat	
	hardwood: free standing: 600 mm wide: 1000 mm high overall: length	
S34	1220 mm	3.15
S35	1500 mm	4.20
S36	2000 mm	6.25

Item		1 Free-standing £	2 Ground-fixed £
	composite concrete/hardwood: 2000 mm long		
S37	600 mm wide: 750 mm high	12.50	20.30
S38	650 mm wide: 850 mm high	15.60	23.40
S39	700 mm wide: 800 mm high	19.50	27.30
S40	galvanised mild steel: 1800 mm long: 550 mm wide: 800 mm high: two fixing points	—	12.75
	Bench		
S41	composite concrete/hardwood: 2000 mm long: 600 mm wide: 450 mm high	11.40	11.75
S42	galvanised mild steel: 1800 mm long: 600 mm wide: 450 mm high: two fixing points	—	11.75
S43	Combined bench/picnic table: softwood or hardwood: not exceeding 2000 mm long	7.50	—

T: Handrails and Balustrades

STEEL ISOLATED TUBULAR HANDRAILS AND BALUSTRADES

Specification
Steel tubes: to BS 1387.

Galvanising: hot dip to BS 729.

Screwed fittings: malleable cast iron to BS 143 and 1256.

Clamp type fittings: from an approved manufacturer.

Method of measurement
Handrail, baluster or the like:
Measure over all fittings.

Rates for the following include
Screwing:
For screws.

Bolting:
For mortices in concrete, brickwork or stonework.

For bolts.

Item		1	2	3	4	5	6
		Light weight				Medium weight	
		Black		Galvanised		Galvanised	
		Nominal size					
		40 mm	50 mm	40 mm	50 mm	40 mm	50 mm
	Metre	£	£	£	£	£	£
T1	Handrail, baluster or the like ...	10.27	12.72	13.02	16.83	14.28	18.49
	Each						
	Extra for						
T2	made bend	8.21	10.96	–	–	–	–
T3	made bend: re-galvanising ...	–	–	18.97	23.67	20.15	24.45
	Extra for welded joint finished smooth						
T4	mitred angle	2.59	3.22	–	–	–	–
T5	intersection	2.06	2.59	–	–	–	–
	Extra for screwed fitting						
T6	straight connector	5.86	7.77	6.34	8.63	6.34	8.63
T7	elbow	6.73	8.44	7.44	9.57	7.44	9.57
T8	tee junction	10.80	14.87	11.75	16.50	11.75	16.50
T9	double tee junction	17.43	24.09	19.31	27.03	19.31	27.03
T10	flange floor plate: bolting	14.99	16.61	16.27	18.34	16.27	18.34

Item	*Metre*	1	2	3	4	5	6
		Light weight				Medium weight	
		Black		Galvanised		Galvanised	
		Nominal size					
		40 mm	50 mm	40 mm	50 mm	40 mm	50 mm
		£	£	£	£	£	£
	Handrail, baluster or the like—*continued*						
	Extra for clamp type fitting						
T11	straight coupling	7.05	8.84	4.94	6.58	4.94	6.58
T12	elbow	7.98	14.51	5.89	12.30	5.89	12.30
T13	side outlet elbow or two socket tee	10.75	13.30	8.67	11.06	8.67	11.06
T14	three socket tee	9.82	16.43	7.73	14.21	7.73	14.21
T15	two socket cross	9.31	14.57	7.21	12.35	7.21	12.35
T16	side outlet tee	10.57	18.48	8.45	16.26	8.45	16.26
T17	four socket cross	15.10	20.34	13.03	18.13	13.03	18.13
T18	light flange: screwing to timber	8.06	10.14	5.97	7.90	5.97	7.90
T19	railing standard flange: bolting ...	16.49	23.17	14.39	20.96	14.39	20.96
	Extra for fitting: welded joints finished smooth						
T20	6 mm flange plate: drilling and screwing to timber	5.19	5.53	—	—	—	—
T21	6 mm flange plate: drilling and bolting	14.64	14.98	—	—	—	—

U: Fencing

GENERALLY

Specification

Concrete post hole filling: 10 N/mm^2: 40 mm maximum aggregate, as specified in the 'Hard Landscaping' Section.

Preservative treatment for softwood: water borne copper chrome arsenic preservative by full-cell pressure treatment to BS 4072. The treatment to be carried out and certified by an approved licensed processor.

Cutting treated timber: re-treat all surfaces to treated timber exposed by cutting, boring etc with matching preservatives applied in two coats by brush.

Holes for supports:

a. Excavate and support earth as necessary.
b. Surround fence support with concrete for half the depth of the hole unless otherwise stated.
c. Backfill to ground level after concrete has hardened with selected excavated material well compacted unless otherwise stated.
d. Dispose of surplus materials.

Definitions

Supports: Posts, struts or the like.

Straining posts: Include end posts and angle posts.

Notes

Components of British Standard fences:
Sizes and materials are stated only where the BS gives alternatives.

Existing holes for supports:
Where existing holes are used no adjustment is to be made to the Rates.

Method of measurement

Height of fence or windbreak:
Measure vertically from surface of ground to top of infilling or to top wire if higher.

Length of fence or windbreak:
Measure over supports.

Rates for the following include

Generally:
For excavating and filling holes for supports.

For supports.

For all cutting including cutting to profile necessary to follow contour of ground.

Setting out to curve:
For setting out to curve straight between posts.

For curve of any radius.

Softwood fencing components and softwood gates:
For preservative treatment.

Taking off, resecuring and fixing only generally:
For component parts of fence of any size or description.

Taking down fence or windbreak complete:
For excavating.

For removing concrete surround to posts and struts and concrete cill.

For reinstating ground with selected excavated material.

Work to old fencing and gates generally:
For taking down supports including excavating, breaking out concrete surround and reinstating ground with selected excavated material.

For excavating and filling holes for supports.

For component parts of fence of any size or description unless otherwise stated.

For removing fixings and fittings.

For providing and fixing nails, staples, stirrups, ties or the like.

For fixing fittings and bolts.

For straining or re-straining.

For cutting, shaping, housing or the like of timber components.

CHAIN LINK FENCING

Specification

Standard chain link fencing: to BS 1722 Part 1.

Length of side of mesh: 50 mm.

Line wire: mild steel.

Steel supports: rolled steel angle: galvanised.

Erection: comply with BS 1722 Part 1, Section 3.

Item	*Metre*	1	2	3	4
		Concrete supports		Steel supports	
		Height			
		900 mm	1200 mm	900 mm	1200 mm
		£	£	£	£
U1	Fence: wire diameter of mesh 3.00 mm: mesh and all wire galvanised	10.68	12.34	10.09	11.68
U2	ADD where wire diameter of mesh 3.55 mm	1.44	2.02	1.44	2.02
U3	Fence: wire diameter of mesh 3.55 mm overall: mesh and wire galvanised and plastics coated Grade A	10.95	13.01	10.35	12.34
U4	ADD where wire diameter of mesh 4.00 mm overall	1.49	1.75	1.49	1.75
	ADD to Items U1 and U3 where				
U5	setting out to curve	0.53	0.53	0.53	0.53
U6	ground sloping exceeding 15° from horizontal	0.53	0.53	0.53	0.53
U7	length not exceeding 3 m	0.53	0.53	0.53	0.53
	Each				
	Extra for straining post				
U8	one strut	19.04	21.88	17.30	18.38
U9	two struts...	33.88	38.47	29.08	31.01

Work to old fencing

Item	*Metre*	£
	Taking down: height not exceeding 1200 mm	
U10	chain link mesh and line wire	1.05
U11	fence complete	3.63
	Fixing only: height not exceeding 1200 mm	
U12	chain link mesh: providing line wire: galvanised or plastics coated	2.52
U13	fence complete	9.17
U14	Resecuring chain link mesh: height not exceeding 1200 mm	1.91

Work to old fencing—*continued*

Item	*Metre*	1 Height 900 mm £	2 Height 1200 mm £
	Supplying only chain link mesh		
U15	galvanised: 3.00 mm diameter wire	3.74	4.83
U16	galvanised: 3.55 mm diameter wire	5.06	6.68
U17	plastics coated Grade A: 3.55 mm overall diameter wire	4.36	5.94
U18	plastics coated Grade A: 4.00 mm overall diameter wire	5.83	7.68
	Each		
	Supplying only		
U19	stretcher bar complete with bolts and cleats	2.84	3.31
U20	winding bracket	1.81	1.81
U21	eye bolt: nuts and washers	0.76	0.76
U22	concrete intermediate post	5.31	6.26
U23	concrete straining post	10.07	11.47
U24	concrete strut	5.05	5.74
U25	steel intermediate post	5.62	6.60
U26	steel straining post	16.75	18.10
U27	steel strut including brace as required	5.82	6.73

Item		1 Intermediate post	2 Straining post: one strut	3 Straining post: two struts	4 Strut
		£	£	£	£
U28	Taking down support	8.70	15.10	21.50	6.52
U29	Fixing only support	10.82	18.00	27.17	9.02

Work to old fencing—*continued*

Item	*Per 10 Metres*	1 Galvanised	2 Plastics-coated Grade A
		£	£
	Line wire		
U30	taking off	1.25	1.25
U31	re-straining	2.20	2.20
U32	fixing only	5.03	5.03
U33	supplying only	1.87	1.95

RABBIT FENCING

Specification

Fence filling:
Galvanised wire: 31 mm mesh size: lightly strained: fixed to posts and strainers with galvanised staples and to line wires with proprietary fixing clips.

Turn bottom 150 mm of mesh at right angles to filling and secure on ground with 300×300×75 mm thick turves (cut from fence base) at 1000 mm centres.

Softwood round, bark stripped posts:
75 mm minimum diameter×1520 mm long, peeled and pointed: preservative treated: driven 430 mm into ground at 3000 mm centres.

Line and jumper wire:
3.15 mm galvanised mild steel.

Item	*Metre*	£
U34	Fence: 1080 mm high	11.19
	ADD where	
U35	setting out to curve	0.53
U36	ground sloping exceeding 15° from horizontal	0.53
U37	length not exceeding 3 m	0.53
	Extra for straining post	
U38	one strut	19.15
U39	two struts	33.11
	Work to old fencing	
	Fence complete: height not exceeding 1200 mm	
U40	taking down	3.72
U41	fixing only	9.20
U42	Resecuring mesh: height not exceeding 1200 mm	1.91

STRAINED WIRE FENCING

Specification

Standard strained wire (stock-proof) fencing: General Pattern to BS 1722 Part 3.

Steel supports: rolled steel angle: galvanised.

Wood supports: sawn softwood, square section.

Line wire: 5 mm diameter galvanised mild steel.

Number of line wires:
a. 3 for 900 mm high fence;
b. 5 for 1050 mm high fence.

Oak gate post: 100 × 50 mm nominal wrought oak post and 40 × 20 mm nominal wrought oak stop. Countersunk bolt to end post with two black bolts 10 mm diameter with washers. Hole through fence end post and gate post.

Erection: comply with BS 1722 Part 3, Section 3.

Item		1	2	3	4	5	6
		Concrete supports		Steel supports		Wood supports	
		Height					
		900 mm	1050 mm	900 mm	1050 mm	900 mm	1050 mm
	Metre	£	£	£	£	£	£
U43	Fence	3.98	4.69	6.87	7.64	6.02	6.60
	ADD where						
U44	setting out to curve	0.53	0.53	0.53	0.53	0.53	0.53
U45	ground sloping exceeding 15° from horizontal	0.53	0.53	0.53	0.53	0.53	0.53
U46	length not exceeding 3 m	0.53	0.53	0.53	0.53	0.53	0.53
	Each						
	Extra for						
U47	straining post: one strut	10.93	17.94	18.69	19.88	5.90	6.15
U48	straining post: two struts	22.80	32.82	29.44	31.45	12.76	13.01
U49	oak gate post	12.49	15.94	12.49	15.94	12.49	15.94

Work to old fencing

Item	*Metre*	£
	Fence complete: height not exceeding 1050 mm	
U50	taking down	2.24
U51	fixing only	2.70

Work to old fencing—*continued*

Item	*Each*	1 Inter-mediate post	2 Straining post one strut	3 Straining post two struts	4 Strut
		£	£	£	£
U52	Taking down support	4.82	10.51	15.54	5.05
U53	Fixing only support	5.42	9.76	15.81	6.02

Item		£
U54	Taking down oak gate post	4.48
	Fixing only oak gate post and stop: providing bolts	
U55	900 mm high	11.14
U56	1050 mm high	14.15

Item		1 Concrete supports Height 900 mm	2 Concrete supports 1050 mm	3 Steel supports 900 mm	4 Steel supports 1050 mm	5 Wood supports 900 mm	6 Wood supports 1050 mm
		£	£	£	£	£	£
	Supplying only						
U57	intermediate post	5.03	5.31	5.62	6.60	2.59	2.81
U58	straining post	6.14	10.84	16.75	18.10	2.85	3.13
U59	strut	4.76	5.05	5.82	6.73	2.59	2.81
U60	oak gate post: oak stop	4.69	5.48	4.69	5.48	4.69	5.48

Item	*Per 10 Metres*	£
	Line wire	
U61	taking off	0.94
U62	re-straining	0.81
U63	fixing only	2.18
U64	supplying only	0.74
	Each	
U65	Supplying only eye bolt: nuts and washers	0.76

CLEFT CHESTNUT PALE FENCING

Specification

Standard cleft chestnut pale fencing: to BS 1722 Part 4.

Spacing between pales:
a. 75 mm for 1050 to 1350 mm high fences;
b. 50 mm for 1500 mm high fence.

Erection: comply with BS 1722 Part 4, Section 3.

Item		1	2	3	4	5	6	7	8
		Concrete supports				Wood supports			
		Height							
		1050 mm	1200 mm	1350 mm	1500 mm	1050 mm	1200 mm	1350 mm	1500 mm
	Metre	£	£	£	£	£	£	£	£
U66	Fence: posts set in concrete	7.21	9.06	9.95	13.25	7.01	8.11	9.86	12.17
	ADD where								
U67	setting out to curve ...	0.53	0.53	0.53	0.53	0.53	0.53	0.53	0.53
U68	ground sloping exceeding 15° from horizontal	0.53	0.53	0.53	0.53	0.53	0.53	0.53	0.53
U69	length not exceeding 3 m...	0.53	0.53	0.53	0.53	0.53	0.53	0.53	0.53
U70	DEDUCT where wood supports pointed and driven	—	—	—	—	1.24	1.50	1.98	2.46
	Each								
	Extra for								
U71	straining post: one strut: pointed and driven	—	—	—	—	15.16	18.16	20.31	23.44
U72	straining post: two struts: pointed and driven	—	—	—	—	27.03	30.22	34.37	39.54
U73	straining post: one strut: set in concrete	20.63	26.71	29.12	30.31	15.16	18.16	20.31	23.44
U74	straining post: two struts: set in concrete	35.95	44.71	46.12	49.17	27.03	30.22	34.37	39.54

Work to old fencing

Item	Metre	1 Support set in concrete £	2 Support driven £
	Taking down: height not exceeding 1500 mm		
U75	fence complete	3.27	2.21
U76	chestnut paling	0.93	0.93

Item		1 Concrete supports 1050 and 1200 mm £	2 Concrete supports 1350 and 1500 mm £	3 Wood supports 1050 and 1200 mm £	4 Wood supports 1350 and 1500 mm £
	Fixing only				
U77	fence complete	3.37	4.48	3.91	6.16
U78	DEDUCT where wood supports pointed and driven	—	—	0.21	0.23
U79	chestnut paling	2.14	2.70	3.16	4.21

Item		£
	Supplying only chestnut paling	
U80	1050 mm high	3.89
U81	1200 mm high	4.30
U82	1350 mm high	4.83
U83	1500 mm high	5.26

Item	Each	1 Intermediate post £	2 Straining post one strut £	3 Straining post two struts £	4 Strut £
	Taking down support				
U84	set in concrete	8.71	15.10	21.50	6.52
U85	driven	1.80	2.76	4.24	1.48
	Fixing only support				
U86	concrete: set in concrete	10.82	18.00	27.04	9.02
U87	wood: pointed and driven	5.47	13.69	19.17	4.57
U88	wood: set in concrete	10.82	17.12	22.59	5.47

Work to old fencing—*continued*

Item	*Each*	1	2	3	4
		Height			
		1050 mm	1200 mm	1350 mm	1500 mm
		£	£	£	£
	Supplying only				
U89	concrete intermediate post	5.90	6.26	6.94	8.90
U90	concrete straining post	7.21	11.47	12.95	14.23
U91	concrete strut	5.05	5.74	6.11	7.16
U92	wood intermediate post	2.51	2.73	3.41	4.59
U93	wood straining post	3.13	3.40	4.27	5.76
U94	wood strut	2.51	2.73	3.41	4.59

Item		£
U95	Supplying only eye bolt: nuts and washers	0.76

CLOSE BOARDED FENCING

Specification

Standard close boarded fencing: to BS 1722 Part 5.

Concrete posts: mortised for arris rails.

Timber posts: for 1800 mm high fence: 125 × 100 × 2550 mm long.

Arris rails: two cut from minimum 75 × 75 mm section.

Wood gravel boards: 32 × 150 mm.

Erection: comply with BS 1722 Part 5, Section 3.

Item	*Metre*	1	2	3	4	5	6
		Softwood boards			Oak pales		
		Height					
		1200 mm	1650 mm	1800 mm	1200 mm	1650 mm	1800 mm
		£	£	£	£	£	£
	Fence: oak posts: concrete gravel board						
U96	softwood rails	27.22	31.85	40.09	—	—	—
U97	oak rails	27.81	32.74	41.56	31.67	39.07	48.22
	ADD where						
U98	with capping and counter rail	3.00	3.00	3.00	3.73	3.73	3.73
U99	setting out to curve	0.53	0.53	0.53	0.53	0.53	0.53
U100	ground sloping exceeding 15° from horizontal	0.53	0.53	0.53	0.53	0.53	0.53
U101	length not exceeding 3 m	0.53	0.53	0.53	0.53	0.53	0.53
U102	DEDUCT where gravel board of same timber as filling	3.05	3.05	3.05	2.59	2.59	2.59

CLOSE BOARDED FENCING

Item	Metre	1	2	3	4	5	6
		Softwood boards			Oak pales		
		Height					
		1200 mm	1650 mm	1800 mm	1200 mm	1650 mm	1800 mm
		£	£	£	£	£	£
	Fence: concrete posts and gravel board						
U103	softwood rails	29.46	34.83	43.33	—	—	—
U104	oak rails	30.06	35.72	44.00	33.93	42.05	51.30
	ADD where						
U105	with capping and counter rail	3.00	3.00	3.00	3.73	3.73	3.73
U106	setting out to curve	0.53	0.53	0.53	0.53	0.53	0.53
U107	ground sloping exceeding 15° from horizontal	0.53	0.53	0.53	0.53	0.53	0.53
U108	length not exceeding 3 m	0.53	0.53	0.53	0.53	0.53	0.53
U109	DEDUCT where gravel board of same timber as filling	3.05	3.05	3.05	2.59	2.59	2.59

Work to old fencing

Item	Metre	1 Taking down	2 Fixing only
		£	£
	Fence complete		
U110	1200 mm high ...	5.07	18.42
U111	1650 mm high ...	6.08	20.47
U112	1800 mm high ...	7.00	22.12
	Fence excluding posts		
U113	1200 mm high ...	3.82	15.22
U114	1650 mm high ...	4.49	18.42
U115	1800 mm high ...	5.05	19.80
U116	Arris rail: detaching or refixing pales ...	0.96	5.45
U117	Capping ...	0.22	0.47
U118	Counter rail ...	0.47	1.40
U119	Gravel board ...	1.00	4.84
	Pale or board: exceeding five pales or boards in groups: (measure fence length)		
U120	1200 mm high ...	1.60	6.65
U121	1650 or 1800 mm high ...	1.91	9.13
	Each		
	Pale or board: isolated or in group not exceeding five pales or boards		
U122	1200 mm high ...	0.31	1.69
U123	1650 or 1800 mm high ...	0.44	2.04

Work to old fencing—*continued*

Item	*Metre*	1 Softwood £	2 Oak £
	Supplying only		
U124	arris rail	0.80	0.97
U125	capping	1.06	1.28
U126	counter rail	0.66	0.71
U127	gravel board	1.24	1.48
U128	pale or board	0.38	0.50

Item		£
U129	Supplying only concrete gravel board	5.07
	Each	
U130	Taking down post	5.26
U131	Fixing only post	8.39

Item		1 Height 1200 mm £	2 1650 mm £	3 1800 mm £
	Supplying only post			
U132	concrete	11.35	15.48	17.54
U133	oak	6.26	8.47	9.61

Item		£
U134	Supplying only bolt: nuts and washers	0.50

WOODEN PALISADE FENCING

Specification

Standard wooden palisade fencing: to BS 1722 Part 6.

Oak posts: 125 × 100 mm.

Arris rails: oak: two cut from minimum 75 × 75 mm section.

Oak palisades:

a. For 1200 mm high fence: 65 × 20 mm rectangular: pointed tops.
b. For 1650 and 1800 mm high fences: triangular: two cut from 50 × 50 mm section: weathered tops.

Erection: comply with BS 1722 Part 6, Section 3.

WOODEN PALISADE FENCING

Item	Metre	1	2	3
		Height		
		1200 mm	1650 mm	1800 mm
		£	£	£
	Fence			
U135	concrete posts	14.69	21.53	23.87
U136	oak posts	15.89	26.14	28.95
	ADD where			
U137	setting out to curve	0.53	0.53	0.53
U138	ground sloping exceeding 15° from horizontal	0.53	0.53	0.53
U139	length not exceeding 3 m	0.53	0;53	0.53

Work to old fencing

		1	2
		Taking down	Fixing only
		£	£
	Fence complete		
U140	1200 mm high	3.85	13.41
U141	1650 mm high	4.79	17.38
U142	1800 mm high	5.77	18.78
	Fence excluding posts		
U143	1200 mm high	2.11	8.48
U144	1650 mm high	2.52	11.17
U145	1800 mm high	3.13	12.48
U146	Arris rail: detaching or refixing palisades	0.94	3.63
	Palisades: exceeding five palisades in groups (measure fence length)		
U147	1200 mm high	0.97	5.72
U148	1650 or 1800 mm high	1.44	8.20
	Each		
	Palisade: isolated or in group not exceeding five palisades		
U149	1200 mm high	0.31	1.67
U150	1650 or 1800 mm high	0.39	2.03
	Metre		
	Supplying only		
U151	arris rail	—	0.89
U152	palisade	—	0.41

	Each	£
U153	Taking down post	5.26
U154	Fixing only post	8.39

Work to old fencing—*continued*

Item	*Each*	1	2	3
		Height		
		1200 mm	1650 mm	1800 mm
		£	£	£
	Supplying only post			
U155	concrete	13.05	17.21	18.73
U156	oak	6.78	9.14	17.03

Item		£
U157	Supply only bolt: nuts and washers	0.50

WOODEN POST AND RAIL FENCING

Specification

Standard wooden post and rail fencing: to BS 1722 Part 7: 1100 mm high.

Erection: comply with BS 1722 Part 7, Section 3.

	Metre	1	2	3	4
		Nailed type		Mortised type	
		Softwood	Oak	Softwood	Oak
		£	£	£	£
	Fence: three rails				
U158	main posts pointed and driven	8.91	13.47	9.71	14.76
U159	main posts set in concrete	6.96	11.06	7.31	12.81
	ADD where				
U160	with four rails	2.63	3.41	4.28	4.90
U161	setting out to curve	0.53	0.53	0.53	0.53
U162	ground sloping exceeding 15° from horizontal	0.53	0.53	0.53	0.53
U163	length not exceeding 3 m	0.53	0.53	0.53	0.53

	Work to old fencing	1	2	3	4	5	6	7	8
		Taking down				Fixing only			
		Softwood		Oak		Softwood		Oak	
		Nailed	Mortised	Nailed	Mortised	Nailed	Mortised	Nailed	Mortised
		£	£	£	£	£	£	£	£
	Fence complete								
U164	three rails	3.07	3.77	3.07	3.77	6.39	7.92	8.19	9.69
U165	four rails	3.55	4.49	3.55	4.49	8.22	10.53	10.78	12.91
U166	Rail	0.48	0.72	0.48	0.72	1.83	2.61	2.60	3.21

WOODEN POST AND RAIL FENCING

Work to old fencing—*continued*

Item	*Each*	1	2	3	4	5	6	7	8
		Taking down				Fixing only			
		Softwood		Oak		Softwood		Oak	
		Nailed	Mortised	Nailed	Mortised	Nailed	Mortised	Nailed	Mortised
		£	£	£	£	£	£	£	£
U167	Prick post: pointed and driven	—	0.76	—	0.76	—	1.49	—	1.49
	Main post								
U168	pointed and driven ...	1.58	1.58	1.58	1.58	4.50	4.50	4.50	4.50
U169	set in concrete ...	5.05	5.05	5.05	5.05	2.20	2.20	2.20	2.20

Item		1	2	3	4
		Supplying only			
		Softwood		Oak	
		Nailed	Mortised	Nailed	Mortised
	Metre	£	£	£	£
U170	Rail	0.80	0.80	1.69	1.69
	Each				
U171	Prick post: 1600 mm long: pointed for driving	1.51	—	3.16	—
U172	Main post: 1800 mm long	4.34	5.20	5.92	6.31
U173	ADD where pointed for driving	0.60	0.60	0.85	0.85

WOVEN WOOD AND LAP BOARDED PANEL FENCING

Specification

Standard woven wood and lap boarded panel fencing: to BS 1722 Part 11.

Lap boarded panels: any type.

Erection: comply with BS 1722 Part 11, Section 3.

Item		1	2	3	4	5	6
		Woven wood panels			Lap boarded panels		
		Height					
		1200 mm	1500 mm	1800 mm	1200 mm	1500 mm	1800 mm
	Metre	£	£	£	£	£	£
	Fence: softwood panels and capping						
U174	softwood posts	16.58	18.11	19.49	15.77	17.01	18.11
U175	oak posts	16.73	18.27	19.67	15.90	17.18	18.30
U176	concrete posts: rectangular or slotted	19.12	21.08	22.65	18.30	19.98	21.27

Item	Metre	1	2	3	4	5	6
		Woven wood panels			Lap boarded panels		
		Height					
		1200 mm	1500 mm	1800 mm	1200 mm	1500 mm	1800 mm
		£	£	£	£	£	£
	Fence: softwood panels and capping—*continued*						
	ADD where						
U177	with cedar panels and capping	11.31	12.14	13.98	10.01	10.56	11.81
U178	setting out to curve	0.53	0.53	0.53	0.53	0.53	0.53
U179	ground sloping exceeding 15° from horizontal	0.53	0.53	0.53	0.53	0.53	0.53
U180	length not exceeding 3 m ...	0.53	0.53	0.53	0.53	0.53	0.53

Work to old fencing

Item		1	2
		Taking down	Fixing only
		£	£
U181	Fence complete: height not exceeding 1800 mm	4.48	7.66
	Each		
U182	Fence panel	2.18	9.04
U183	Capping	0.58	1.19
U184	Post	5.26	8.39

Item	*Metre*	£
	Supply only capping	
U185	softwood	1.41
U186	cedar	3.06

Item	*Each*	1	2	3
		Height		
		1200 mm	1500 mm	1800 mm
		£	£	£
	Supplying only panel			
	softwood			
U187	woven wood	14.00	16.44	17.66
U188	lap boarded	12.18	14.00	14.62
	cedar			
U189	woven wood	35.99	40.27	45.57
U190	lap boarded	31.32	34.32	37.73
	Supplying only new post			
U191	softwood	2.81	3.29	3.76
U192	oak	3.86	4.51	5.16
U193	concrete: rectangular or slotted	6.66	7.79	8.90
U194	Supplying only bolt: nuts and washers	0.60	0.60	0.60

TEMPORARY WINDBREAKS

Specification

Netting: high density polyethylene. Obtain from an approved manufacturer:

a. 7 mm round mesh; protection factor of 60%.
b. 30×2 mm mesh; protection factor of 55%.

Supports: softwood; maximum 75 mm diameter, at approximately 1500 mm centres, driven 450 mm into ground.

Fixing: wiring or stapling to supports.

Rates for the following include

Generally:
For extra supports at intersections.

Item	*Metre*	1 7 mm round mesh Height 1500 mm £	2 30×2 mm mesh 2000 mm £
U195	Windbreak	7.85	12.50
	ADD where		
U196	setting to curve	0.55	0.55
U197	ground sloping exceeding 15° from horizontal	0.55	0.55
U198	length not exceeding 3 m	0.55	0.55
U199	Taking down windbreak complete	1.05	1.25

FENCE CLADDING

Specification

Fence cladding: polyethylene mesh: from an approved manufacturer:

a. high density: black or green: 25×5 mm mesh aperatures;
b. medium density: black: 4 mm diamond mesh aperatures.

Rates for the following include

Generally:
For fixing to wooden fences with galvansied staples or galvanised tying wire.

For fixing to wire or metal fences with galvanised tying wire.

Item	*Square Metre*	£
	Fence cladding	
U200	high density	4.30
U201	medium density	4.12

ISOLATED TIMBER POSTS TO PREVENT VEHICLE ACCESS

Rates for the following include

Generally:
For filling holes for posts with concrete to the full depth.

Item	*Each*	£
U202	Oak post: 150 × 100 mm: 1200 mm long overall: weathered top: setting 750 mm in ground ...	22.65

GATES AND POSTS FOR CHAIN LINK FENCING

Specification

Gates and posts generally: to BS 1722 Part 1.

Steel gates:

a. Steel formed with rectangular hollow section outside frame members and braces, size 40 × 40 × 3 mm; galvanised to BS 729 after manufacture.

b. Chain link mesh infill to match fencing fixed with stretcher bars and bolts.

c. Complete with fittings for hanging and securing.

Steel gate posts: rectangular hollow section galvanised to BS 729 after manufacture. Complete with fittings for hanging and securing.

Rates for the following include

Generally:
For filling posts holes with concrete to the full depth.

		1	2	3
		Width		
		1000 mm	1500 mm	2000 mm
	Each	£	£	£
	Steel gate: any type of mesh: single or double			
U203	900 mm high ...	248.91	275.92	302.92
U204	1200 mm high ...	262.00	294.78	327.54
U205	1400 mm high ...	275.09	313.64	352.16

		1	2	3	4
		Concrete		Steel	
		125 × 125 mm	150 × 150 mm	80 × 80 × 3.6 mm	100 × 100 × 4 mm
		£	£	£	£
	Post: hanging or shutting: fence height				
U206	900 mm ...	20.69	—	20.45	—
U207	1200 mm ...	24.02	28.70	21.89	27.87
U208	1400 mm ...	27.02	32.38	26.33	34.82

CLOSE BOARDED GATES

Specification

Timber: wrought softwood or sawn oak.

Stiles, rails and braces: size 65 × 65 mm. Gates exceeding 1200 mm high to have a centre rail.

Board/pale filling: size 90 × 13 mm tapered to 6 mm. Lap 13 mm and nail to rails and braces with rose-headed composition nails.

Item	*Each*	1 Softwood £	2 Oak £
U209	Framed and braced gate: not exceeding 1.00 m²	41.83	46.99
U210	ADD *for each additional 0.30 m²*	5.85	6.57

WOODEN PALISADE GATES

Specification

Timber: wrought softwood or sawn oak.

Nails: galvanised.

Nominal sizes of timber members:

Member	Width of gate not exceeding 900 mm	Width of gate exceeding 900 mm
	mm	mm
Stile	50 × 75	65 × 75
Rail	32 × 75	45 × 75
Brace	32 × 83	45 × 83
Pale—pointed	20 × 90	20 × 90

Fix pales to rails and braces with nails. Space pales 75 mm apart.

Item	*Each*	1 Softwood £	2 Oak £
U211	Framed and braced gate: not exceeding 1.00 m²	37.00	44.02
U212	ADD *for each additional 0.30 m²*	6.17	8.06

FIELD GATES AND POSTS

Specification

Field gates and posts generally: to BS 3470.

Timber gates: framed, braced and bolted. Bolts, nuts and washers galvanised to BS 729.

Steel gates: framed, braced and welded, heavy duty. Galvanised to BS 729 after manufacture. Complete with fittings for hanging and securing.

Timber posts: weathered tops. Holes for ironmongery.

Steel posts: capped tops. Completed with fittings for hanging and securing.

Rates for the following include

Generally:
For filling holes for posts with concrete to the full depth.

Item	Each	1 Wrought softwood £	2 Sawn oak £	3 Steel £
	Gate			
U213	2400 × 1100 mm	76.51	85.99	88.72
U214	3000 × 1100 mm	88.78	99.63	102.95
U215	3600 × 1100 mm	101.08	113.27	117.22

Item	Each	1 Wrought softwood £	2 Sawn oak £	3 Concrete £	4 Circular hollow section steel £
	Gate post				
U216	175 × 175 × 2100 mm long	26.98	33.61	33.93	—
U217	200 × 200 × 2100 mm long	34.92	43.58	44.00	—
U218	89 mm diameter × 2100 mm long	—	—	—	35.25
U219	114 mm diameter × 2100 mm long	—	—	—	45.90
U220	Gate stop: 100 × 125 × 600 mm: mortice for bolt socket	7.16	7.88	—	—

IRONMONGERY FOR GATES

Specification

Ironmongery: steel, galvanised to BS 729.

Note

Ironmongery fixed partly to softwood and partly to hardwood:
Measure as fixed to hardwood.

Rates for the following include

Generally:
For providing ironmongery complete with screws, bolts, nuts and washers.

For holes and mortices in timber.

IRONMONGERY FOR GATES

Item	Each	1 Fixing to Softwood £	2 Hardwood £
	Pair of hook and band hinges		
U221	300 mm: bolting hook through post	8.36	9.11
U222	450 mm: building in hook to brickwork	13.25	13.98
U223	450 mm: heavy patern: building in hook to brickwork	16.68	17.42
U224	Set of double strap hinges for field gate: to BS 3470	31.12	32.49
U225	Barrel bolt: 150 mm	3.82	4.19
U226	Gate latch: 50 mm: automatic pattern	2.35	2.58
U227	Gate spring catch and hook plate: 500 mm	16.74	17.85
U228	Cabin hook and eye: 150 mm	4.66	5.35

WORK TO OLD GATES AND POSTS

Item	Each	£
	Taking down	
U229	gate: not exceeding 1 m^2	6.16
U230	ADD *for each additional 1 m^2*	3.01
U231	gate post	6.16
	Fixing only	
U232	gate: not exceeding 1 m^2	10.40
U233	ADD *for each additional 1 m^2*	3.72
U234	gate post: filling hole completely with concrete	4.06

CLEARING FENCE LINES

Item	Metre	£
U235	Clearing areas not exceeding 1.00 m wide, to each side of fence line, of bushes, scrub or undergrowth: cutting long grass, weeds, brambles, saplings not exceeding 150 mm girth or the like: disposing arisings: prior to erecting fence	2.42

PERGOLAS AND ARCHES

Specification

Softwood round or square bark-stripped members:
Butt jointed and fixed together with galvanised nails or bolts.

Rates for the following include

Generally:
For setting support posts into ground at depth ordered.

For filling holes for support posts with hardcore well packed and consolidated to half the full depth and backfilling the remainder with selected excavated material to the full depth.

For all cutting and notchings.

For treating cut timber and ends of support posts with preservative.

Item	*Each*	£
	Softwood: 100 mm diameter or 100 × 100 mm square	
	support post	
U236	not exceeding 2000 mm long	10.61
U237	2000 to 4000 mm long	13.66
	Metre	
U238	vertical, horizontal or diagonal member	3.30

BREAKING THROUGH PAVINGS

Item	*Each*	£
	Extra over excavating for support for breaking through existing paving not exceeding 150 mm thick and reinstating	
U239	concrete	0.55
U240	reinforced concrete	0.83
U241	brick, block or stone or concrete flag	0.30
U242	coated macadam or asphalt	0.38

V: Decorative and Preservative Coatings

GENERALLY

Specification

Materials:
Obtain from an approved manufacturer.

Workmanship:
Comply with Sub-Sections 43, 44, 45 and 46 of Section 5 of BS 6150 unless otherwise ordered.

Preparation of surfaces:
Prepare in accordance with the coating manufacturer's recommendations as appropriate to the surface to be covered.

Definitions

General surfaces: All surfaces *except* glazed windows or doors and railings, fences or gates.

Irregular: Corrugated, fluted, panelled, carved or ornamental.

Plain open railing, fence or gate: Includes plain post and wire, post and rail, cleft pale, palisade and metal bar.

Close railing, fence or gate: Includes close boarded and corrugated.

Method of measurement

Generally:
Measure the area or girth covered and make allowance for the extra girth of edges, mouldings, panels, sinkings, corrugations, flutings, carvings, enrichments or the like unless otherwise stated.

Make no deduction for voids not exceeding 0.50 m².

Plain open railing, fence or gate:
Measure the area painted.

Close railing, fence or gate:
Measure each side overall.

Rates for the following include

Generally:
For external work.

For any area or girth unless otherwise stated.

For all necessary preparatory work.

For application by brush, roller or spray.

For providing dust sheets, tarpaulins, etc to protect adjacent works.

Isolated areas:
For work of any girth.

OIL PAINTING: METAL

Specification

General use oil paint: undercoat and hard-gloss finish.

Item		1	2	3	4	5	6
		Painting one undercoat and one finishing coat on new work delivered primed	Painting one coat primer, one undercoat and one finishing coat on new work	Painting one finishing coat on old painted work	ADD for each additional undercoat	ADD for one coat etching primer	ADD for one coat rust inhibitor
	Square Metre	£	£	£	£	£	£
	General surfaces						
V1	exceeding 300 mm girth	3.45	5.58	2.86	1.44	1.43	1.48
V2	ADD where to perforated surfaces—*per side*	1.05	1.69	0.86	0.44	0.43	0.45
V3	exceeding 300 mm girth: irregular	3.60	5.91	2.95	1.53	1.51	1.57
	Metre						
V4	isolated surfaces not exceeding 300 mm girth	1.41	2.27	1.16	0.58	0.56	0.60
	Each						
V5	isolated areas not exceeding 0.50 m²	2.34	3.80	1.94	0.99	0.97	1.02
	Square Metre						
	Plain open railings, fences or gates						
V6	exceeding 300 mm girth	3.86	6.24	3.18	1.53	1.52	1.59
	Metre						
V7	isolated surfaces not exceeding 300 mm girth	1.39	2.25	1.14	0.56	0.55	0.58
	Each						
V8	isolated areas not exceeding 0.50 m²	2.32	3.75	1.91	0.92	0.91	0.95
	Square Metre						
V9	Close railings, fences or gates: exceeding 300 mm girth	3.62	5.84	2.98	1.43	1.42	1.47

BITUMINOUS PAINTING: METAL

Specification

Bituminous paint: black bitumen solution for cold application to BS 3416 Type 1.

Item		1 Painting one coat bituminous paint on old painted work	2 Painting one coat primer and one coat bituminous paint on new or old untreated work	3 ADD for each additional coat of bituminous paint
	Square Metre	£	£	£
	General surfaces			
V10	exceeding 300 mm girth	1.97	2.91	1.17
V11	ADD where to perforated surfaces—*per side*	0.60	0.89	0.35
V12	exceeding 300 mm girth: irregular	2.05	3.02	1.22
	Metre			
V13	isolated surfaces not exceeding 300 mm girth	0.73	1.07	0.43
	Each			
V14	isolated areas not exceeding 0.50 m^2	1.22	1.79	0.72
	Square Metre			
	Plain open railings, fences or gates			
V15	exceeding 300 mm girth	2.21	3.28	1.32
	Metre			
V16	isolated surfaces not exceeding 300 mm girth	0.79	1.17	0.47
	Each			
V17	isolated areas not exceeding 0.50 m^2	1.33	1.97	0.79
	Square Metre			
V18	Close railings, fences or gates: exceeding 300 mm girth	2.08	3.08	1.24

ALUMINIUM PAINTING: METAL

Item		1 Painting one coat aluminium paint on old painted work	2 Painting one coat primer and one coat aluminium paint on new or old untreated work	3 ADD for each additional coat of aluminium paint
	Square Metre	£	£	£
	General surfaces			
V19	exceeding 300 mm girth	2.28	3.55	1.53
V20	ADD where to perforated surfaces—*per side*	0.76	1.07	0.47
V21	exceeding 300 mm girth: irregular	2.62	3.73	1.58
	Metre			
V22	isolated surfaces not exceeding 300 mm girth	0.96	1.35	0.59
	Each			
V23	isolated areas not exceeding 0.50 m^2	1.59	2.25	0.97
	Square Metre			
	Plain open railings, fences or gates			
V24	exceeding 300 mm girth	2.81	3.96	1.70
	Metre			
V25	isolated surfaces not exceeding 300 mm girth	1.02	1.42	0.61
	Each			
V26	isolated areas not exceeding 0.50 m^2	1.69	2.37	1.02
	Square Metre			
V27	Close railings, fences or gates: exceeding 300 mm girth	2.64	3.71	1.60

MICACEOUS IRON OXIDE PAINTING: METAL

Item		1 Painting one coat micaceous iron oxide on old painted work	2 Painting one coat primer and one coat micaceous iron oxide on new or old untreated work	3 ADD for each additional coat of micaceous iron oxide
	Square Metre	£	£	£
	General surfaces			
V28	exceeding 300 mm girth	3.55	4.72	2.21
V29	ADD where to perforated surfaces—*per side*	1.07	1.43	0.68
V30	exceeding 300 mm girth: irregular	3.70	4.91	2.30
	Metre			
V31	isolated surfaces not exceeding 300 mm girth	1.28	1.69	0.80
	Each			
V32	isolated areas not exceeding 0.50 m^2	2.14	2.83	1.33
	Square Metre			
	Plain open railings, fences or gates			
V33	exceeding 300 mm girth	3.95	5.25	2.47
	Metre			
V34	isolated surfaces not exceeding 300 mm girth	1.42	1.90	0.89
	Each			
V35	isolated areas not exceeding 0.50 m^2	2.37	3.15	1.48
	Square Metre			
V36	Close railings, fences or gates: exceeding 300 mm girth	3.71	4.92	2.33

OIL PAINTING: WOOD

Specification

General use oil paint: undercoat and hard-gloss finish.

Item		1 Painting one coat primer, one undercoat and one finishing coat on new work	2 Painting one finishing coat on old painted work	3 ADD for each additional undercoat
	Square Metre	£	£	£
	General surfaces			
V37	exceeding 300 mm girth	5.16	2.35	1.22
	Metre			
V38	isolated surfaces not exceeding 300 mm girth	1.86	0.84	0.44
	Each			
V39	isolated areas not exceeding 0.50 m^2	3.10	1.41	0.73
	Square Metre			
	Plain open railings, fences or gates			
V40	exceeding 300 mm girth	5.77	2.63	1.36
	Metre			
V41	isolated surfaces not exceeding 300 mm girth	2.08	0.95	0.49
	Each			
V42	isolated areas not exceeding 0.50 m^2	3.46	1.58	0.81
	Square Metre			
V43	Close railings, fences or gates: exceeding 300 mm girth	5.40	2.46	1.28

PRESERVATIVE PAINTING: WOOD

Specification

Creosote for brush application: to BS 3051.

Wood preservative for subsequent painting: copper naphthenate solution to BS 5056 Type 1.

Item		1	2	3	4	5	6
		Painting one coat creosote on		ADD for each additional coat of creosote	Painting one coat preservative on		ADD for each additional coat of preservative
		new or old untreated work	old treated work		new or old untreated work	old treated work	
	Square Metre	£	£	£	£	£	£
V44	General surfaces: exceeding 300 mm girth	1.49	1.34	0.88	1.51	1.39	1.24
V45	Plain open railings, fences or gates: exceeding 300 mm girth	1.79	1.61	1.05	1.81	1.68	1.48
V46	Close railings, fences or gates: exceeding 300 mm girth	1.68	1.50	0.99	1.70	1.58	1.39
	Metre						
	General surfaces or plain open railings, fences or gates						
V47	isolated surfaces not exceeding 300 mm girth	0.64	0.58	0.38	0.65	0.61	0.54
	Each						
V48	isolated areas not exceeding 0.50 m²	1.07	0.97	0.63	1.09	1.01	0.89

OILING: WOOD

Specification

Oil:

a. Raw linseed oil for hardwood: to BS 243.
b. Mineral oil for teak.

Item	*Square Metre*	1 Twice oiling new work	2 Washing down and twice oiling old work
		£	£
	General surfaces		
V49	exceeding 300 mm girth	2.71	2.32
	Metre		
V50	isolated surfaces not exceeding 300 mm girth	0.98	0.83
	Each		
V51	isolated areas not exceeding 0.50 m²	1.63	1.39

STAINING: WOOD

Specification

Stain:

Exterior wood impregnation preservative stain.

Item	*Square Metre*	1 Staining with one coat of wood stain on old stained work	2 Staining with two coats of wood stain on new or old untreated work	3 ADD for each additional coat of stain
		£	£	£
	General surfaces			
V52	exceeding 300 mm girth	1.33	2.08	0.77
	Metre			
V53	isolated surfaces not exceeding 300 mm girth	0.47	0.75	0.28
	Each			
V54	isolated areas not exceeding 0.50 m²	0.79	1.25	0.46

SEALER VARNISHING: WOOD

Specification

Sealer varnish: oleo-resinous sealer.

Item		1	2
		Varnishing with one coat sealer varnish on new or old untreated work	ADD for each additional coat of sealer varnish
	Square Metre	£	£
	General surfaces		
V55	exceeding 300 mm girth	1.65	1.27
	Metre		
V56	isolated surfaces not exceeding 300 mm girth	0.60	0.45
	Each		
V57	isolated areas not exceeding 0.50 m²	0.99	0.76

POLISHING: WOOD

Specification

Wax polish: bleached beeswax and genuine turpentine or a proprietary product.

Item		1	2	3	4
		Sealing and polishing new work	Cleaning and reviving old work	Stripping and repolishing old work	ADD for staining or bleaching old work
	Square Metre	£	£	£	£
	General surfaces				
V58	exceeding 300 mm girth	14.62	12.76	23.72	1.71
	Metre				
V59	isolated surfaces not exceeding 300 mm girth	5.26	4.59	8.54	0.62
	Each				
V60	isolated areas not exceeding 0.50 m²	8.77	7.65	14.23	1.03

W: Drainage

GENERALLY

Reference to other Sections: The Preambles to the following Sub-Sections of the 'Hard Landscaping' Section apply equally to this Section unless otherwise stated:

Excavating and Filling
In situ Concrete
Brickwork

Specification

Jointing pipes of dissimilar materials: ensure that:
a. pipe materials are compatible; or
b. a suitable adaptor is used.

Connection to Local Authority's and Water Company's sewers: make arrangements with the Local Authority/Water Company for connections to be made.

Interim and final pipeline tests: either water or air test:

a. Water test as follows:
   1. effectively temporarily plug drain under test;
   2. connect standpipe to head of drain under test;
   3. fill pipes with water approximately one hour before starting test;
   4. apply a test pressure of not less than 1200 mm head of water above crown of the pipes at the high end of the section being tested but not more than 6000 mm above the low end;
   5. non-absorbent pipes: make good after 10 minutes loss of water indicated by a fall in level. After 30 minutes, no further measurable loss to be evident;
   6. absorbent pipes: make good loss of water indicated by a fall in level and measure over a period of 30 minutes by adding water from a measuring vessel at regular intervals of 10 minutes. Record the quantity required to maintain the original water level. In interim tests the average quantity added must not exceed one litre per hour per metre diameter of pipe eg:
   0.05 litre per metre of 100 mm diameter pipe in 30 minutes;
   0.08 litre per metre of 150 mm diameter pipe in 30 minutes;
   0.12 litre per metre of 225 mm diameter pipe in 30 minutes;
   0.15 litre per metre of 300 mm diameter pipe in 30 minutes;
   0.19 litre per metre of 375 mm diameter pipe in 30 minutes;
   0.22 litre per metre of 450 mm diameter pipe in 30 minutes.
   In final tests pipelines will be considered satisfactory if, after stabilisation, water level shows no appreciable fall after 30 minutes.

b. Air test as follows:
   1. effectively temporarily plug drain under test;
   2. connect glass 'U' tube gauge to drain plug in length of drain under test at a convenient position;
   3. pump or blow air into test section until pressure equivalent to 100 mm head of water is indicated;
   4. where gullies are connected, pump or blow air into test section until pressure equivalent to 50 mm head of water only is indicated;
   5. without further air being added, the pressure must not fall below 75 mm after a period of 5 minutes. Where gullies are connected, pressure must not fall below 38 mm after a period of 5 minutes.

   If pipeline fails this test, apply water test as (a).

Interim test of underground chambers: apply interim test for watertightness before backfilling and before surrounding precast manholes with concrete as follows:

a. keep external faces of chambers clear of backfill for inspection until approved;
b. temporarily seal all pipe openings in chambers;
c. fill chambers less than 1.5 m in depth to invert to the underside of the cover and deeper chambers to a minimum depth of 1.5 m with clean water and allow up to 8 hours for initial absorption. Top up before starting test;
d. the water level should not drop over a period of 30 minutes in excess of figures in the following Table:

Age of chamber construction up to Water Test Level	Method of Construction		
	Brickwork	Concrete sections	Clayware, plastics or any 'One Piece' Chambers
	Maximum permissible drop in water level (mm)		
3 to 7 days only	40	10	5
over 31 days	5	5	5

Where the drop in level during a water test on a brick manhole or inspection chamber exceeds 40 mm but does not exceed 60 mm, the test may be repeated at 31 days, when the criteria of acceptance for that period shall apply.

Final test of underground chambers: apply final test as specified for interim test except that external faces will not be exposed for inspection.

Definition

Manhole: Includes manholes, catchpits, soakaways and petrol/mud/oil interceptors.

Note

Generally:
Rates in other Sections apply to drainage where Rates are not given in this Section.

Method of measurement

Pipework:
Measure over all fittings and branches.

Reducing fittings:
Measure extra over the largest pipe in which they occur.

Rates for the following include

Generally:
For testing new drainage work.

Pipe:
For horizontal or vertical pipe in trench.

For joints in the running length.

For work in runs of any length unless otherwise stated.

Pipe fitting:
For cutting and jointing pipes to fitting.

Taper or the like:
For socket at small end.

Accessory:
For jointing to drain.

For jointing as pipework unless otherwise stated.

For setting on and surrounding with 150 mm concrete grade 20 N/mm^2: 20 mm aggregate including formwork.

For extra excavation, disposal and earthwork support.

Work to existing pipework and manholes:
For removing and replacing gratings, manhole covers or the like.

For temporarily stopping drains.

SURFACE WATER DRAINAGE

EXCAVATING TRENCHES

Specification

Excavation: excavate to required levels with accurate and even gradients restricting trench widths to either 450 mm or 1.5 times external diameter of pipe to be laid plus 250 mm, whichever is the greater.

Selected backfill: backfill and compact by hand in 100 mm layers to 300 mm above pipes not requiring a surround with approved selected fill readily compacted, free from roots, vegetable matter, building rubbish, frozen soil, clay lumps retained on a 75 mm sieve and stones retained on a 25 mm sieve.

Main backfill: backfill with previously excavated material excluding boulders, timber, vegetable matter and waste material in layers not exceeding 300 mm thick and compact each layer.

Method of measurement

Excavating trench:
Measure uninterrupted line of excavating between manholes or between an accessory and a manhole or between accessories.

Rates for the following include

Generally:
For earthwork support.

For consolidating trench bottom.

For trimming excavations.

For forming handholes.

For backfilling and compacting.

For setting aside and replacing topsoil.

For disposing surplus excavated materials.

Item	*Metre*	1	2	3	4	5
		Nominal size of pipe				
		not exceeding 200 mm	225 mm	300 mm	375 mm	450 mm
		£	£	£	£	£
	Excavating trench: for pipe: average depth					
W1	not exceeding 0.25 m	1.08	—	—	—	—
W2	0.25 to 0.50 m	2.95	3.12	3.58	—	—
W3	0.50 to 0.75 m	5.29	5.60	6.45	7.18	—
W4	0.75 to 1.00 m	8.03	8.50	9.76	10.88	11.89
W5	1.00 to 1.25 m	11.09	11.74	13.49	15.03	16.41
W6	1.25 to 1.50 m	14.44	15.29	17.56	19.56	21.36
W7	1.50 to 1.75 m	18.05	19.11	21.95	24.45	26.70
W8	1.75 to 2.00 m	21.90	23.18	26.64	24.51	32.39
W9	2.00 to 2.25 m	25.97	27.48	31.58	35.17	38.41
W10	2.25 to 2.50 m	30.24	32.01	36.78	40.96	44.73

W11 Where hand excavation is specifically ordered, multiply the foregoing Rates by 2.00.

GRANULAR MATERIAL

Specification

Granular material: coarse aggregate to BS 882 Part 4, single size or graded.

Lay granular material and compact in 100 mm layers. Do not lay granular material within 24 hours of the completion of concrete beds.

Beds: full width of trench: 100 mm thick.

Haunching: side fill half way up the pipe.

Surrounds: thickness above pipe equal to nominal pipe size.

Item	*Metre*	1 Bed £	2 Bed and haunching £	3 Bed and surround £
	For pipe: nominal size			
W12	not exceeding 200 mm	2.99	3.93	8.74
W13	225 mm	4.03	5.14	11.53
W14	300 mm	5.13	6.48	14.30
W15	375 mm	7.84	9.71	24.17
W16	450 mm	8.82	10.95	30.26

Item	*Cubic Metre*	£
W17	Thickening to bed or surround	49.49

PLAIN IN SITU CONCRETE

Specification

Concrete mix: grade 20 N/mm^2: 20 mm aggregate.

Beds: 300 mm wider than external diameter of pipe: 150 mm thick.

Haunching: side fill half way up the pipe and slope off to the crown.

Surrounds: 150 mm thick above pipe.

Vertical casing: 150 mm thick.

Compressible joint filler: bitumen impregnated insulating board to BS 1142 Part 3, 18 mm minimum thick, cut to finished profile of concrete and pipe.

Construction joints: form at intervals not exceeding 5000 mm coinciding with pipe joints.

Rates for the following include

Generally:
For formwork.

Pipes with flexible joints:
For construction joints through concrete.

Item		1	2	3	4	5	6
		Pipes with rigid joints			Pipes with flexible joints		
		Bed and haunching	Bed and surround	Vertical casing	Bed and haunching	Bed and surround	Vertical casing
	Metre	£	£	£	£	£	£
	For pipe: nominal size						
W18	80 mm	8.14	13.35	19.89	8.97	14.58	21.12
W19	100 mm	9.23	13.93	23.24	10.14	16.41	23.66
W20	150 mm	11.35	18.69	27.38	12.47	20.37	29.06
W21	200 mm	13.45	22.53	32.90	14.67	24.34	34.59
W22	225 mm	14.43	24.42	36.72	15.88	26.60	38.17
W23	300 mm	17.85	31.18	45.58	19.53	33.70	48.10
W24	375 mm	21.93	39.82	57.08	23.94	42.83	59.08
W25	450 mm	23.94	45.86	65.96	27.18	49.83	68.62
	Cubic Metre						
W26	Thickening to bed or surround ...	96.77	98.28	125.84	100.70	102.28	132.96

DRAINAGE CHANNELS TO PAVED AREAS

Specification

Polyester concrete drainage channel units and fittings: from an approved manufacturer:

a. Dimensions: 155 mm wide overall: 105 to 309 mm deep overall: 100 mm bore; channel with integral fall.
b. Joint type: in accordance with the manufacturer's recommendations.
c. Gratings: cast iron slotted inlay gratings fixed with bolts and locking bars.
d. Lay on 100 mm concrete (20 N/mm^2: 40 mm maximum size aggregate) base and haunch up with similar concrete both sides.

Precast concrete drainage units and fittings: from an approved manufacturer:

a. Dimensions: 310 mm wide overall: 230 mm deep: encasing 110 mm diameter PVC pipe.
b. Joint type: in accordance with the manufacturer's recommendations.
c. Inlets: single row of circular conical or straight slotted inlet apertures.
d. Lay on 100 mm concrete (20 N/mm^2: 40 mm maximum size aggregate) base and haunch up with similar concrete both sides.

Note

Excavation, etc:
Pay for at the Rates for excavating trenches for pipes.

Rates for the following include

Generally:
For concrete bed, haunching and formwork.

Polyester concrete drainage channel units:
For units of any depth within manufacturer's range.

Item		£
	Metre	
W27	Polyester concrete drainage channel: grating	52.80
	Each	
	Extra for	
W28	end plate	4.44
W29	end plate with 100 mm diameter PVC union	7.17
	PVC union: to suit knock out drainage point	
W30	100 mm diameter: round	2.69
	150 mm diameter	
W31	round	6.47
W32	oval	6.76
	Metre	
W33	Precast concrete drainage units	55.97
	Each	
	Extra for	
W34	junction or silt box: removable grating	55.30
W35	rodding unit: lockable removable grating	34.65

CONCRETE PIPEWORK

Specification

Pipes and fittings: to BS 5911 and manufactured by a BSI Kitemark Licensee:

a. Pipe class: M.
b. Cement type: ordinary Portland.
c. Ogee rigid joint type: cement and sand mortar (1:2).
d. Spigot and socket joint type: in accordance with the pipe manufacturer's recommendations.

		1	2	3	4	5	6
		Ogee joints			Spigot and socket flexible joints		
		Nominal size					
		300 mm	375 mm	450 mm	300 mm	375 mm	450 mm
Item	*Metre*	£	£	£	£	£	£
W36	Pipe	15.97	21.71	27.14	19.16	26.06	32.55
	Each						
	Extra for						
W37	taper: any size socket	—	—	—	27.35	35.29	43.45
W38	bend	26.78	36.39	47.59	39.02	41.82	55.72
	junction: any type						
W39	100 mm branch	30.39	30.39	30.39	30.39	30.39	30.39
W40	150 mm branch	39.94	39.94	39.94	39.94	39.94	39.94
W41	225 mm branch	55.62	55.62	55.62	55.62	55.62	55.62
W42	300 mm branch	74.96	74.96	74.96	74.96	74.96	74.96

CLAY PIPEWORK: RIGID JOINTS

Specification

Spigot and socket pipes and fittings: to BS 65 and manufactured by a BSI Kitemark Licensee;

a. Type: surface water extra strength.
b. Joint type: cement and sand mortar (1:2).

CLAY PIPEWORK: RIGID JOINTS—*continued*

Item		1	2	3
		Nominal size		
		100 mm	150 mm	225 mm
	Metre	£	£	£
W43	Pipe	6.83	11.07	20.60
	Each			
	Extra for			
W44	pipe stopper: setting in mortar	4.19	5.61	10.99
W45	taper	—	11.26	22.57
W46	level invert taper	—	10.84	21.72
W47	bend	3.24	5.29	13.30
W48	junction: any type: any size branch	5.81	9.54	—

CLAY PIPEWORK: FLEXIBLE JOINTS

Specification

Pipes and fittings: to BS 65 and manufactured by a BSI Kitemark Licensee:

a. Type: normal.

b. Joint type: in accordance with the pipe manufacturer's recommendations.

c. Strength class: super strength.

		1	2	3	4	5	6
		Plain ended pipes			Spigot and socket pipes		
		Nominal size					
		100 mm	150 mm	225 mm	100 mm	150 mm	225 mm
	Metre	£	£	£	£	£	£
W49	Pipe	4.94	8.67	14.49	6.98	8.96	16.89
	Each						
	Extra for						
W50	adaptor to plastics pipe	4.76	7.57	—	6.73	7.82	—
W51	pipe stopper: setting in mortar	3.87	6.00	—	5.47	6.20	—
W52	taper	—	6.74	22.03	—	6.97	25.68
W53	bend	3.81	7.91	26.01	5.38	8.17	30.32
W54	junction: any type: any size branch	7.11	13.91	29.66	9.27	15.45	33.78
W55	double junction: any type: any size branches	—	—	—	18.18	31.42	69.01

PLASTICS PIPEWORK

Specification

UPVC pipes and fittings: to BS 4660 and manufactured by a BSI Kitemark Licensee: joint type: ring seal.

Item		1	2
		Nominal size	
		110 mm	160 mm
	Metre	£	£
W56	Pipe	4.72	8.14
	Each		
	Extra for		
W57	taper	—	11.23
W58	bend	7.53	13.35
W59	junction: any type: any size branch	9.13	20.64
W60	double junction: any type: any size branches	9.45	23.99

WORK TO EXISTING PIPEWORK: CONCRETE

		1	2	3
		Nominal size		
		300 mm	375 mm	450 mm
	Each	£	£	£
W61	Connecting new pipe to existing pipe end: cement joint	19.61	29.80	35.51

		1	2	3	4
		Nominal size			
		100 mm	150 mm	225 mm	300 mm
		£	£	£	£
W62	Connecting new pipe to existing pipe: cutting away concrete bed and haunching: cutting aperture: saddle connector: cement joints: making good concrete bed and haunching	43.15	57.87	86.93	138.02

WORK TO EXISTING PIPEWORK: CLAY

Item	Each	1 Nominal size 100 mm £	2 150 mm £	3 225 mm £	4 300 mm £
	Connecting new pipe to existing pipe end				
W63	cement joint	7.41	8.36	10.71	16.06
W64	double socket: cement joints	15.45	21.38	39.39	62.68
W65	Cutting out short length of existing pipe and concrete bed and haunching: inserting new oblique branch: loose collar: cement joints: making good concrete bed and haunching	30.90	44.05	72.12	113.77
W66	Connecting new pipe to existing pipe: cutting away concrete bed and haunching: cutting aperture: saddle connector: cement joints: making good concrete bed and haunching	51.51	72.98	98.30	128.72

CLAY ACCESSORIES

Specification

Terminal fittings: to BS 65 and manufactured by a BSI Kitemark Licensee.

Item	Each	£
	Gully: outlet 100 mm nominal size	
W67	225 mm diameter	61.77
W68	150 × 150 mm...	39.66
W69	230 × 230 mm...	68.99
	ADD to Items W68 and W69 for	
W70	horizontal inlet	10.26
W71	vertical inlet	10.26
W72	Trap: for use with raising piece: 100 mm diameter: outlet 100 mm nominal size	19.31
W73	Raising piece: 225 mm diameter: 150, 230 or 305 mm high	15.30
W74	Trapless yard gully: 225 mm diameter × 380 mm deep: outlet 100 mm nominal size ...	54.91
W75	Hopper: 225 to 100 mm diameter: 230 mm high	22.73
	ADD to Items W73 to W75 for	
W76	horizontal inlet	21.34
W77	vertical inlet	21.34

CLAY ACCESSORIES—*continued*

Item	*Each*	£
	Road gully: trapped: outlet 100 or 150 mm nominal size	
W78	300 mm diameter × 610 mm deep	72.97
W79	300 mm diameter × 760 mm deep	79.38
W80	375 mm diameter × 760 mm deep	97.76
W81	375 mm diameter × 915 mm deep	115.83
W82	450 mm diameter × 915 mm deep	131.63
W83	ADD for rodding eye and stopper	8.39
	Grease or mud intercepting gully: outlet 100 mm nominal size	
W84	225 mm diameter × 550 mm deep	71.31
W85	225 mm diameter × 610 mm deep: galvanised perforated bucket	98.63
W86	300 mm diameter × 610 mm deep: galvanised perforated bucket	124.08
W87	ADD for horizontal inlet	27.03
W88	ADD for rodding eye and stopper	6.71

PLASTICS ACCESSORIES

Specification
UPVC terminal fittings: in accordance with pipe manufacturer's recommendations.

Item	*Each*	£
	Gully: plastics grating: outlet 110 mm nominal size	
W89	180 mm diameter: roddable	20.45
W90	180 mm diameter: roddable: 110 mm diameter back inlet	20.97
W91	ADD for back inlet bend	2.47
W92	Trap: for use with raising piece: 110 mm diameter: outlet 110 mm nominal size	3.91
	Raising piece: 110 mm diameter	
W93	155 mm high: two 82 mm boss upstands	3.71
W94	180 mm high: four 50 mm boss upstands	5.25
	Hopper: 140 mm high: four back inlet upstands: plastics grating	
W95	160 × 160 mm to 110 mm diameter	21.98
W96	230 × 160 mm to 110 mm diameter	22.78

CAST IRON ACCESSORIES

Specification

Road gully gratings and frames: to BS 497 Part 1 and manufactured by a BSI Kitemark Licensee.

Rates for the following include

Generally:
For coated fittings unless otherwise stated.

Item	*Each*	1 Coated £	2 Galvanised £
	Grating		
W97	40 mm thick: to suit 225 mm diameter gully or raising piece	6.43	9.16
W98	55 mm thick: to suit 300 mm diameter gully or raising piece	11.85	20.03
W99	150 × 150 mm	2.82	3.76
W100	230 × 230 mm	6.28	9.22
W101	240 × 140 mm	4.08	9.07

Item		£
	Road gully grating and frame: bedding and flaunching in cement and sand mortar	
W102	heavy duty non-rock type: wheel load 11.50 tonnes: minimum waterway area 900 cm^2	86.24
W103	heavy duty hinged type: wheel load 11.50 tonnes: minimum waterway area 650 cm^2	67.13
W104	medium duty hinged type: wheel load 5.00 tonnes: minimum waterway area 650 cm^2	58.74
W105	kerb-type for use in kerbs of half or full batter profile: weir depth 115 mm	92.22

ACCESSORIES: SUNDRIES

Specification

Engineering bricks: imperforate clay bricks to BS 3921 Class B.

Item	*Metre*	1 100 × 100 mm £	2 100 × 150 mm £
W106	Plain concrete: grade 20 N/mm²: 20 mm aggregate: kerb to gully top: trowelled finish: rounded top: angles: dishing to grating: formwork	9.62	10.95

Item		£
W107	Brick seating to frame of road gully: engineering bricks in cement and sand mortar (1:3): half-brick thick: two courses high: facework one side: (including the cost of bricks) ...	12.48

WORK TO EXISTING ACCESSORIES

Rates for the following include

Raising or lowering gully grating and frame:
For taking off and re-setting grating and frame.

For any excavation etc in lowering level.

For any materials etc in raising level.

Item	*Each*	£
W108	Raising or lowering gully grating and frame: any size—*per 75 mm of level difference* ...	14.86
W109	Taking up and replacing grating: not exceeding 350 mm diameter or 250 × 250 mm ...	1.57
W110	ADD where fixed with screws	1.01
W111	Taking up grating: cutting away bedding mortar and taking up frame: not exceeding 350 mm diameter or 250 × 250 mm	3.14
W112	Fixing only frame: bedding in cement and sand mortar (1:3): replacing grating: not exceeding 350 mm diameter or 250 × 250 mm	4.66
W113	Taking up grating: burning or cutting out joint and removing frame: not exceeding 350 mm diameter or 250 × 250 mm	6.46
W114	Fixing only frame: caulked lead joint: replacing grating: not exceeding 350 mm diameter or 250 × 250 mm	23.14
	Taking up road gully grating and frame: cutting away mortar: overall area	
W115	not exceeding 0.10 m²	6.46
W116	0.10 to 0.25 m²	8.02
W117	0.25 to 0.50 m²	16.11
	Fixing only road gully grating and frame: bedding and flaunching in approved quickset resin mortar: overall area	
W118	not exceeding 0.10 m²	5.82
W119	0.10 to 0.25 m²	12.14
W120	0.25 to 0.50 m²	17.85

TESTING EXISTING DRAINS

Rates for the following include

Generally:
For taking up and replacing in position gratings, manhole covers or the like.

For carrying out final test in accordance with the requirements for new work.

Item	*Metre*	£
	Testing with water or air: existing drain: diameter	
W121	not exceeding 200 mm	0.46
W122	200 to 350 mm	0.81
W123	350 to 500 mm	1.13

CLEARING EXISTING DRAINS

Item	*Each*	1 Distance between access points not exceeding 30 m £	2 30 to 50 m £
	Rodding drain from manhole or cleaning eye: cleaning out and removing all matter: flushing with water and leaving clear: removing and replacing in position manhole covers or the like: diameter		
W124	not exceeding 200 mm	18.80	25.06
W125	200 to 350 mm	26.63	33.67

Item		£
	Cleaning out and removing all mud and rubbish	
W126	from gully: any type	4.13
W127	from catchpit	5.22
W128	ADD to Items W126 and W127 where mud bucket taken out and cleaned and replaced in position	1.55

LAND DRAINAGE

GENERALLY

Note

Generally:
Rates in other Sections apply to land drainage where Rates are not given in this Sub-Section.

EXCAVATING TRENCHES

Rates for the following include

Generally:
For backfilling with hard rubble, gravel, broken stone or clinker graded 75 to 40 mm to within 150 mm of ground level and covering with selected topsoil.

Item	*Metre*	1	2	3
		Nominal size of pipe		
		not exceeding 200 mm	225 mm	300 mm
		£	£	£
	Excavating trench: for pipe: average depth			
W129	0.25 to 0.50 m	9.56	9.66	9.79
W130	0.50 to 0.75 m	15.66	17.10	18.54
W131	0.75 to 1.00 m	21.84	24.00	26.16
W132	1.00 to 1.25 m	24.98	26.57	28.22
W133	1.25 to 1.50 m	29.66	32.75	36.05

CONCRETE PIPEWORK

Specification

Pipes: to BS 1194; plain ended, unjointed.

Item	*Metre*	1	2	3
		Nominal size		
		100 mm	150 mm	225 mm
		£	£	£
	Pipe			
W134	non-porous inverts	4.94	6.28	9.63
W135	porous inverts	6.70	8.03	10.56

CLAY PIPEWORK

Specification
Pipes: to BS 1196; plain ended or socketed, unjointed.

Item	Metre	1	2	3	4
		Nominal size			
		75 mm	100 mm	150 mm	225 mm
		£	£	£	£
W136	Pipe	2.47	2.83	4.12	6.13

PLASTICS PIPEWORK

Specification
Pipes: BS 4962 and manufactured by a BSI Kitemark Licensee. Joint in accordance with pipe manufacturer's recommendations.

Rates for the following include
Pipe:
For junctions and fittings.

Item	Metre	£
	Pipe	
	smooth, perforated, plain ended and unjointed: nominal size	
W137	110 mm	5.95
W138	160 mm	10.27
	flexible, corrugated, perforated: jointing: nominal size	
W139	60 mm	0.78
W140	80 mm	1.24
W141	100 mm	1.76
W142	125 mm	3.58
W143	160 mm	5.79

MOLE DRAINAGE

Specification

Mole drain areas at depths, spacings and directions ordered.

Implements: use a mole plough with expander drawn by a tractor, fitted with tracks if so directed. Set plough to provide a smooth channel of circular cross section at the required depth.

Timing: carry out the work only when subsoil is moist enough to enable a smooth channel to be formed, and when the surface is dry enough to avoid damage to the soil structure.

Rolling: on completion of the work roll the surface with a tractor-drawn roller, or run the tracks of the tractor drawing the plough along the surface slit so as to press back the soil.

Item	*100 Metres*	£
W144	Forming mole drain: not exceeding 75 mm diameter × 500 mm deep	13.65

STONE FILLED OPEN CHANNELS

Item	*Metre*	£
W145	Excavating open channel in short lengths: 150 to 250 mm wide × 300 mm deep to follow fall of ground: filling to within 50 mm of surface with approved hardcore and top 50 mm with approved fine gravel	3.25

OUTFALLS

Notes

Brick headwalls:
Calculate the number of bricks from the Table on Page 84.

Concrete work:
Pay for the Rates for in situ concrete in the 'Hard Landscaping' Section.

Item	*Each*	£
	Excavating for land drain outfall headwall and 1 m of pipe not exceeding 150 mm diameter: backfilling: headwall size	
W146	500 × 800 mm	6.83
W147	600 × 1000 mm	8.19
W148	750 × 600 mm	7.17
W149	900 × 750 mm	8.73
	Outfall comprising glass reinforced cement headwall with rot proof netting anchor and 1 m rigid polythene pipe: cutting hole in headwall: jointing pipe to headwall and land drain pipe	
	500 × 800 mm headwall: pipe diameter	
W150	80 mm	18.20
W151	100 mm	18.53
W152	150 mm	19.11

OUTFALLS—*continued*

Item	*Each*	£
	Outfall comprising glass reinforced cement headwall—*continued*	
	600 × 1000 mm headwall: pipe diameter	
W153	100 mm	30.88
W154	150 mm	32.50
W155	200 mm	34.78
	Outfall comprising one brick headwall in any type of bricks in cement and sand mortar (1:3): brick on edge coping: facework to face, two returns and top: cutting and fitting around and building in pipe end: (*excluding* cost of bricks)	
	750 × 600 mm headwall: pipe diameter	
W156	80 mm	38.07
W157	100 mm	40.24
W158	150 mm	42.53
W159	200 mm	44.34
W160	225 mm	57.36
	900 × 750 mm headwall: pipe diameter	
W161	80 mm	51.05
W162	100 mm	53.21
W163	150 mm	55.50
W164	200 mm	57.31
W165	225 mm	70.33

DITCHING

GENERALLY

Specification

Spoil: throw well clear of ditch and spread and level either by grading out into the adjoining land or forming a bank with smooth even sides and top as directed.

Work to bottoms: commence from the outfall and work upstream so that the bottom falls to an even gradient and is 75 mm below the invert of pipes and culverts.

EXCAVATING AND RE-GRADING DITCHES

Specification

Excavate to re-form ditches and re-grade bottoms to falls as directed. Finish work 75 mm below and 75 mm clear on either side of culverts or pipes in the ditch's course.

Courses: to be of even width and even grade and as straight as possible. Any curves to be smooth and free flowing.

Drains: bring in other open drains discharging into the ditch so as to give the minimum resistance to the flow. Clear ends of drain pipes discharging into the ditch and make good any damage.

Channel spaces: leave channel spaces to allow surface water from the adjoining land to reach the ditch where required.

Note

Actual volume for excavating:
Agree with the SO before work commences.

EXCAVATING AND RE-GRADING DITCHES—*continued*

Item	*Cubic Metre*	£
W166	Excavating to re-form ditch: re-grading bottom: removing, spreading and levelling spoil: including work to drains and channel spaces: removing and disposing all vegetation and rubbish: leaving waterway clear ...	9.26
W167	Excavating to form ditch: grading bottom: removing, spreading and levelling spoil: including work to drains and channel spaces ...	5.75

CLEARING WATERWAYS

Note

Where silt has accumulated to a greater depth than 150 mm, or falls of earth have occurred, obstructing the course of the ditch, measure clearance in accordance with Item W166.

Item	*Metre*	£
	Clearing bottoms: removing all silt not exceeding 150 mm deep, vegetation and rubbish: disposing arisings: leaving waterway clear	
W168	channel: not exceeding 610 mm girth ...	1.00
W169	culvert: not exceeding 1200 mm girth ...	3.30
	Each	
W170	Cleaning grating to culvert mouth: not exceeding 1200 mm diameter: disposing arisings: leaving waterway clear ...	5.30

CLEARING DITCH SIDES

Notes

Protection of habitats:
Carry out all work with due regard to the protection of wild life habitat. To satisfy this requirement, clear only one bank side per annum, the other side being cleared in alternate years.

Vegetation traps:
Where vegetation is being cut on the banks or weeds removed from the bottom, erect vegetation traps just upstream of the next culvert or pipe below the work to collect all vegetation floating downstream. Clear traps frequently to prevent backing up.

Item	*Square Metre*	£
W171	Cutting all vegetation other than trees on banks of ditch: removing and depositing arisings ...	0.20
	ADD for	
W172	burning arisings ...	0.05
W173	disposing arisings ...	0.10

MANHOLES AND SOAKAWAYS

EXCAVATING

Rates for the following include

Generally:

For forming sides curved on plan if ordered.

For setting aside and replacing topsoil.

For backfilling with and compacting selected excavated material in layers not exceeding 150 mm thick.

For disposing surplus excavated materials.

Item	Cubic Metre	1 Maximum depth not exceeding 1.00 m £	2 2.00 m £	3 4.00 m £
W174	Pit	25.71	30.19	36.12

Item	Square Metre	£
W175	Levelling bottom of excavation: compacting	0.27

EARTHWORK SUPPORT

Item	Square Metre	1 Maximum depth not exceeding 1.00 m £	2 2.00 m £	3 4.00 m £
	To face of excavation: distance between opposing faces			
W176	not exceeding 2 m	2.63	3.05	3.61
W177	2 to 4 m	2.80	3.42	4.56
W178	exceeding 4 m	4.89	6.31	8.32
W179	ADD where curved	1.57	1.78	2.06

HARDCORE

Specification

Hardcore for soakaways: broken brick, stone or crushed concrete 150 to 75 mm gauge, containing no fines.

Item	Cubic Metre	£
W180	Filling to or around soakaway: exceeding 0.25 m average thick	19.06

IN SITU CONCRETE: PLAIN

Item	*Cubic Metre*	£
W181	Backfilling around manhole or the like: 20 N/mm²: 20 mm aggregate	94.00
	Square Metre	
	Benching in bottom: trowelled finish: 20 N/mm²: 14 mm aggregate: average thickness	
W182	225 mm ...	36.43
W183	300 mm ...	48.64
W184	375 mm ...	60.72

IN SITU CONCRETE: SULPHATE-RESISTING: PLAIN

	Cubic Metre	£
	Bed: 30 N/mm²: 20 mm aggregate	
W185	not exceeding 150 mm thick ...	84.01
W186	150 to 450 mm thick ...	75.77

IN SITU CONCRETE: SULPHATE-RESISTING: REINFORCED

Note

Reinforcement:
Pay for at the appropriate Rates in the 'Hard Landscaping' Section.

	Cubic Metre	£
	Suspended slab: tamped finish: 30 N/mm²: 20 mm aggregate	
W187	not exceeding 150 mm thick ...	118.07
W188	150 to 450 mm thick ...	112.06
W189	exceeding 450 mm thick ...	108.03

FORMWORK

Item	*Square Metre*	£
W190	Soffit of slab: any height: not exceeding 200 mm thick	23.13
W191	ADD *for each additional 100 mm of thickness*	1.79
	Metre	
	Edge of suspended slab	
W192	not exceeding 250 mm high	7.62
W193	250 to 500 mm high	11.54
W194	Extra for rebate—*per 25 mm of girth*	0.70

		1	2	3
		Diameter		
		300 mm	375 mm	450 mm
		£	£	£
W195	Half-round channel: fine finish: to falls	8.70	13.05	17.42
W196	ADD where curved on plan	2.90	4.35	5.92
	Each			
W197	Extra for junction between branch channel and main channel ...	2.30	2.89	3.48

PRECAST CONCRETE: SULPHATE-RESISTING

		1	2
		20 N/mm²: 20 mm aggregate	30 N/mm²: 20 mm aggregate
	Square Metre	£	£
W198	Cover slab: 100 mm thick (measure reinforcement separately)	24.56	26.09
W199	ADD *for each additional 25 mm of thickness*	5.52	5.87

	Each	£
W200	Extra for rebated opening for manhole cover and frame: any size: any thickness	16.74

PRECAST CONCRETE UNITS

Specification

Manholes: to BS 5911 and manufactured by a BSI Kitemark Licensee; joints for watertight construction in accordance with manufacturer's recommendations.

Step irons: to BS 1247, fixed in manhole components before delivery.

Soakaways: perforated concrete to BS 5911 and manufactured by a BSI Kitemark Licensee; joints in accordance with manufacturer's recommendations.

Rates for the following include

Generally:
For bedding and pointing in cement and sand mortar (1:3).

For manhole or soakaway units (measure soakaway perforations separately).

Cover slab:
For reinforcement.

Shaft, chamber and taper rings:
For unreinforced units not exceeding 1200 mm diameter.

For reinforcement in units 1350 mm diameter.

Item	Each	1	2	3	4	5
		Internal diameter				
		675 mm	900 mm	1050 mm	1200 mm	1350 mm
		£	£	£	£	£
	Cover slab: opening 525 mm minimum diameter					
W201	75 mm thick	28.79	46.37	55.57	76.43	91.77
W202	88 mm thick	29.66	45.01	57.27	78.74	94.61
W203	125 mm thick	32.12	48.72	62.01	85.28	102.43
	Shaft ring					
W204	300 mm high	32.14	—	—	—	—
W205	600 mm high	51.50	—	—	—	—
	Chamber ring					
W206	300 mm high	—	41.51	48.15	56.50	—
W207	600 mm high	—	60.36	74.16	90.23	155.53
W208	900 mm high	—	73.65	93.22	115.36	212.18
	Taper ring: 675 mm minimum diameter					
W209	600 mm high	—	67.57	82.40	107.43	—
W210	900 mm high	—	—	—	—	175.10

Item	Each	1	2	3
		Height		
		150 mm	230 mm	300 mm
		£	£	£
	Rectangular shaft section: internal size			
W211	600 × 450 mm	30.90	33.48	36.05
W212	750 × 600 mm	35.79	39.24	42.95
W213	1000 × 675 mm	43.21	47.23	51.81

PRECAST CONCRETE UNITS—*continued*

Item	*Each*	£
W214	Reducing unit: internal size 1000×675 mm reducing to 750×600 mm ...	93.32
	Cover slab: 75 mm thick: minimum clear opening 600×450 mm: to suit shaft section	
W215	600×450 mm	38.11
W216	750×600 mm	65.25

Item		1	2	3	4	5	6	7	8	9
		Diameter								
		50 mm	80 mm	100 mm	150 mm	200 mm	225 mm	300 mm	375 mm	450 mm
		£	£	£	£	£	£	£	£	£
W217	Perforation through shaft, chamber ring or the like: for pipe or as soakaway perforation ...	1.85	3.04	4.06	6.08	8.14	9.12	12.15	15.24	18.23

Item		£
W218	Step iron: cast into concrete during manufacture ...	3.32

PLASTICS UNITS

Specification

Inspection chambers: polypropylene, compatible with the pipe system.

Rates for the following include

Generally:
For jointing to drains.

For fixing blanking plugs.

For setting on and surrounding with 150 mm concrete grade 20 N/mm²: 20 mm aggregate including formwork.

For extra excavation, disposal and earthwork support.

Item	*Each*	£
	Inspection chamber: 450 mm internal diameter: 110 mm nominal size channels and side inlets: blanking plugs: cast iron cover Grade C light duty single seal type and plastics frame: depth to invert	
W219	230 mm ...	53.86
W220	600 mm ...	88.65
W221	1000 mm	106.97

LAYING ONLY BRICKWORK

Specification

Clay common bricks: solid bricks to BS 3924, durability designation FL.

Engineering bricks: imperforate clay bricks to BS 3921 Class B.

Mortar:
Cement and sand (1:3).

Note

Number of bricks:
Calculate the number of bricks from the Table on Page 84.

Rates for the following include

Building in end of pipe:
For cutting pipe.

For turning single half-brick ring arch over pipes 225 to 300 mm nominal size.

For turning double half-brick ring arch over pipes 375 or 450 mm nominal size.

Item	*Square Metre*	1 Common bricks £	2 Engineering bricks £
	Wall: bedding in mortar with open vertical joints		
W222	half-brick thick	17.14	—
W223	one-brick thick	34.33	—
	Wall		
W224	half-brick thick	18.81	23.12
W225	one-brick thick	36.27	43.98
W226	one-and-a-half-brick thick	53.51	65.00
W227	one-brick thick: curved on plan not exceeding 2 m radius	43.52	54.73
W228	one-brick thick: curved on plan not exceeding 2 m radius: 35 mm open vertical joints in alternate courses	41.13	—
	Extra for facework		
W229	exceeding half-brick wide	2.22	2.98
W230	exceeding half-brick wide: curved on plan not exceeding 2 m radius	2.78	3.56

BRICKWORK SUNDRIES

Item	*Each*	1 80 mm £	2 100 mm £	3 150 mm £	4 200 mm £	5 225 mm £	6 300 mm £	7 375 mm £	8 450 mm £
		Nominal size							
	Building in end of pipe: common brickwork: making good facework one side								
W231	half-brick thick	1.78	2.74	3.70	4.39	5.07	6.03	6.99	7.94
W232	one-brick thick	2.34	3.42	4.56	5.47	11.98	14.61	24.65	29.21
W233	one-and-a-half-brick thick	3.42	4.80	6.16	7.70	14.61	16.66	30.81	37.20

W234 Building into engineering brickwork: price at the foregoing Rates for common brickwork multiplied by 2.00.

BRICKWORK SUNDRIES—*continued*

Item	*Metre*	£
	Brick seating to frame of manhole cover: in cement and sand mortar (1:3): facework one side: (including the cost of bricks)	
	half-brick thick: two courses high	
W235	common bricks	10.15
W236	engineering bricks	12.48
	one-brick thick: one course high	
W237	common bricks	8.62
W238	engineering bricks	10.61

CHANNELWORK

Specification

Vitrified clay channels and bends: to BS 65 and manufactured by a BSI Kitemark Licensee:
a. Type: normal.
b. Bed and joint type: cement and sand mortar (1:2).

UPVC channels and bends: to BS 4660 and manufactured by a BSI Kitemark Licensee:
a. Joint type: ring seal.
b. Bed: cement and sand mortar (1:2).

		1	2	3	4	5
		Clay			UPVC	
		Nominal size				
		100 mm	150 mm	225 mm	110 mm	160 mm
	Each	£	£	£	£	£
	Half round section: not exceeding 600 mm effective length					
W239	straight	5.52	7.88	10.82	8.64	11.55
W240	ADD *for each additional 150 mm of effective length*	1.17	1.67	2.83	1.83	2.44
W241	curved	10.30	13.57	32.52	14.20	20.35
W242	ADD *for each additional 150 mm of effective length*	2.19	2.94	7.45	3.03	4.40
	tapering to smaller size					
W243	straight	13.02	26.30	58.28	—	—
W244	curved	14.74	42.48	83.99	—	—
W245	Half section branch bend	4.89	8.63	27.10	9.37	14.45
W246	Three quarter section branch bend	8.85	14.31	48.49	—	—

CAST IRON COVERS AND ACCESSORIES

Specification

Covers and frames: to BS 497 and manufactured by a BSI Kitemark Licensee.

Step irons for brick manholes: to BS 1247 and manufactured by a BSI Kitemark Licensee.

Rates for the following include

Access covers and frames:
For coated units.

For rectangular overall shape to medium and heavy duty frames.

Item	*Each*	£
	Access cover and frame: bedding frame in cement and sand mortar (1:3): bedding cover in grease and sand	
	Grade A: heavy duty non-rock type: minimum clear opening	
W247	550 mm diameter	150.06
W248	600 mm diameter	161.01
	Grade B: medium duty non-rock type: minimum clear opening	
W249	550 mm diameter	94.22
W250	600 mm diameter	91.53
	Grade B: medium duty single seal type: minimum clear opening	
W251	550 mm diameter	97.07
W252	600 × 450 mm	97.36
W253	600 × 600 mm	115.00
	Grade B: medium duty single seal recessed top type: minimum clear opening	
W254	600 × 450 mm	97.36
W255	600 × 600 mm	119.30
	Grade C: light duty single seal type: minimum clear opening	
W256	600 × 450 mm	33.15
W257	600 × 600 mm	62.25
	Grade C: light duty single seal recessed top type: minimum clear opening	
W258	600 × 450 mm	58.50
W259	600 × 600 mm	81.25
W260	ADD to Items W247 to W253 for ventilated cover	17.34
	Set of malleable lifting keys	
W261	for heavy or medium duty covers	7.00
W262	for light duty covers	5.65
	Step iron: building into joints of brickwork	
	general purpose pattern	
W263	115 mm tail	6.37
W264	230 mm tail	6.89
W265	corner pattern: 25 mm diameter: 595 mm long	6.50

STEEL COVERS

Specification

Covers and frames: zinc coated steel, suitable for wheel loadings not exceeding 5 tonnes.

Rates for the following include

Concrete filling to skeleton type manhole covers: For all necessary formwork.

Item	*Each*	1 Clear opening 450 × 600 mm £	2 600 × 600 mm £
	Access cover and frame: bedding frame in cement and sand mortar (1:3): bedding cover in grease and sand		
	floor plate type		
W266	single seal	22.09	28.89
W267	double seal	38.00	50.69
W268	recessed skeleton, non-locking type	36.73	48.92
	ADD where		
W269	locking type	12.08	12.77
W270	locking type with rubber seals	44.39	54.40
W271	ADD for filling with 25 N/mm^2 concrete trowelled smooth	5.20	7.48

WORK TO EXISTING MANHOLES/SOAKAWAYS

Rates for the following include

Raising or lowering cover and frame:
For any excavation etc in lowering level.

For any materials etc in raising level.

Item	*Metre*	£
	Preparing top of existing brick wall for raising	
W272	half-brick thick	1.29
W273	one-brick thick	2.30
W274	one-and-a-half-brick thick	3.58

WORK TO EXISTING MANHOLES/SOAKAWAYS—*continued*

Item	*Each*	1	2	3	4	5	6	7	8
		Nominal size							
		100 mm	110 mm	150 mm	160 mm	225 mm	300 mm	375 mm	450 mm
		£	£	£	£	£	£	£	£
	Cutting out short length of existing pipe and concrete bed and haunching or surround: providing and inserting connector to receive half round section channel (measure channel separately): jointing to pipe in cement and sand mortar (1:2)								
W275	concrete pipe	31.47	—	44.08	—	70.23	98.31	108.15	137.74
W276	plastics pipe	—	12.65	—	15.55	—	—	—	—
W277	clay pipe	15.40	—	18.49	—	34.17	55.61	—	—

Item		1	2	3	4
		Nominal size			
		100 m	150 mm	225 mm	300 mm
		£	£	£	£
W278	Cutting out existing branch drain and branch channel from existing manhole: making good brickwork, rendering and benching	21.63	26.63	32.96	41.79
W279	Connecting new branch drain to existing manhole: cutting hole in wall one-brick thick: cutting away existing benching as necessary: inserting new clay branch bend: bedding and jointing in cement and sand mortar (1:2) making good all work disturbed	38.47	46.74	70.99	89.64

Item		1	2
		Cover and frame: any type: any size: total weight	
		not exceeding 150 kg	150 to 230 kg
		£	£
W280	Taking up and replacing cover: sealing cover in grease	3.81	4.79
W281	Taking up cover: cutting away bedding mortar and taking up frame	6.95	9.27
W282	Fixing only cover and frame: bedding frame in approved quickset resin mortar: bedding cover in grease and sand	7.21	11.33

Item		£
W283	Raising or lowering cover and frame: any size—*per 75 mm of level difference*	19.01

Index

Printed in the United Kingdom for HMSO
Dd291076 6/91 C16 G3392 10170